A "must" for every ~~pastor~~ ... ~~Spirit~~ for
this decade and bey~

Paul Yonggi Cho
(pastor of world's largest church—625,000 people—in Seoul, Korea)

Foundational reading for everyone interested in the church growth movement.

Dale E. Galloway
(pastor of New Hope Community Church, Portland, Oregon, which has grown from 0 to 6,000 in the last 19 years)

One of the most significant books I've ever read.

Lyman Coleman
(founder/director of Serendipity, one of nation's largest publishers of Bible study materials)

Proven strategies that can set churches free!

Bill Hybels
(founding pastor of nation's second-largest church, Willow Creek Community Church, S. Barrington, Illinois, with an attendance of 14,000)

Carl George's penchant for penetrating the maze of theories about church growth, and cutting to the gut of the matter, sets him apart.

Jack W. Hayford
(author, hymn writer and pastor of Church on the Way, Van Nuys, California, a church with 10,000 in average weekly attendance)

No pastor—whether struggling or successful—can afford to ignore the wealth of wisdom packed into these pages.

David A. Hubbard
(president of Fuller Theological Seminary, Pasadena, California, the nation's largest interdenominational seminary)

Carl George is one of the best consultants in the country.

John Maxwell
(author, popular conference speaker, and pastor of the 3,000-person Skyline Wesleyan Church in greater San Diego, California)

A watershed book that must be read and prayed over by pastors and people.

John W. Reed
(chairman, department of pastoral ministries, Dallas Theological Seminary, one of the nation's largest nondenominational seminaries)

The best introduction to the Protestant church in North America in the twenty-first century.

> *Lyle E. Schaller*
> *(author of numerous best-selling books and a nationally recognized church growth consultant)*

One of those *must* books for every progressive pastor.

> *Paul L. Walker*
> *(pastor of Mt. Paran Church of God, Atlanta, Georgia, the nation's tenth-largest church with an attendance of 9,000)*

The most significant step forward in church-growth theory and practice since Donald McGavran wrote the basic textbook . . . in 1970.

> *C. Peter Wagner*
> *(author of numerous best-selling books; Donald A. McGavran Professor of Church Growth, Fuller Theological Seminary, Pasadena, California)*

A truly international model for the church.

> *Terry Walling*
> *(director, Church Resource Ministries, Victoria, Australia)*

Prepare
Your
Church
for the
Future

Carl F. George

Fleming H. Revell
A Division of Baker Book House Co
Grand Rapids, Michigan 49516

Scripture quotations in this book are taken from the Holy Bible, New International Version. Copyright © 1973, 1978, 1984 International Bible Society. Used by permission of Zondervan Bible Publishers.

Meta-Globe, Meta-Zone, Center for Development of Leadership for Ministry, The Docent Project, and The Meta-Church Project are trademarks.

By Carl F. George:
Prepare Your Church for the Future

By Carl F. George and Robert Logan:
Leading and Managing Your Church

By Carl F. George with Warren Bird:
How to Break Growth Barriers

Library of Congress Cataloging-in-Publication Data

George, Carl F.
   Prepare your church for the future / Carl F. George
      p.   cm.
   Includes bibliographical references and index.
   ISBN 0-8007-5365-8
      1. Church work. 2. Christianity—21st century. I. Title
BV4400.G46   1991
250—dc20   91-3827
                                                                                    CIP

First Printing (Oct. 1991), Second Printing (Dec. 1991)
Third Printing (Mar. 1992), Fourth Printing (May 1992)
Fifth Printing (Aug. 1992), Sixth Printing (Oct. 1992)
Seventh Printing (Dec. 1993)

Copyright © 1992 by Carl F. George
Published by Fleming H. Revell
a division of Baker Book House Company
P.O. Box 6287, Grand Rapids, MI 49516-6287

Printed in the United States of America

Acknowledgments

I must make several acknowledgments.

First to Grace, my wife, who for three decades has endured the stream of frequently unanswerable questions and obscure conjecturings that are an inescapable part of a journey of discovery.

Then to Peter Wagner, my mentor, whose enthusiastic appreciation of the good in every Christian tradition has inspired me to maintain a learner's attitude and glean insight from every part of God's universal church.

Also, to those clients who, in entrusting their challenges, problems, and questions to my scrutiny, have helped me far more than they can know. My "systems" view of churches is a synthesis of the gracious contribution and stimulation of many people.

As I've reflected on the contribution of other leaders and authors who've contributed to my understanding, I realize I'd need a separate volume to credit everyone. A special thanks to the following group, whom I could never rank by importance, and who have lighted some facet of Christ's church for me: Verle Ackerman, Jere Allen, Win and Chip Arn, George Barna, Bob Buford, Terry Camsey, Paul Yonggi Cho, Fred Clark, Robert Clinton, Lyman Coleman, Don Cousins,

W. A. Criswell, Des Cummings, Jim Dethmer, John deVries, Jack Dinsbeer, Peter Drucker, Robert W. Erhard, Ed Faulkner, Dan Fuller, Dale Galloway, Eddie Gibbs, Paul Hiebert, Paul Keineke, Jon Heugli, David Hubbard, George Hunter, Karen Hurston, Bill Hybels, Jack Hyles, Mike Jaffarian, Al Janney, Bob Jones, Sr., Ross Juneau, Charles Kraft, Larry Lea, Bob Logan, David Luecke, Duane Mau, John Maxwell, Donald McGavran, Ralph Neighbour, J. Edwin Orr, Paul Pierson, Dan Reeves, Charles Ridley, Arlin Rothauge, Elmer Rund, Pete Scazzero, Lyle Schaller, Mel Schell, Robert H. Schuller, Fred Smith, Jr., Howard Snyder, Chuck Swindoll, J. V. Thomas, Frank Tillapaugh, Elmer Towns, Wayne Van Gelderen, John Vaughan, Rick Warren, Norm Whan, John Wimber, Ralph Winters, Tom Wolf, David Womack, Flavil Yeakley, Jr., and others whose contributions are recalled in flashes.

Finally, thanks to Warren Bird for his smoothing rewrites and reorganizations and to others who did everything from typing to managing the Charles E. Fuller Institute: Joe Webb, Jerome Smith, Diane Wallace, Karan Banando, Bernie Muth, Vince Rutherford, Mae Douglas, and Doug Slaybaugh.

Contents

Section IV: What to Visualize for the Big Picture

Section V: Where to Go From Here

Foreword

The book you hold in your hand is one of a kind.

I know this sounds trite and a little bit like I am attempting to provide some hype for the book just because Carl George is one of my best personal friends. Admitting that I am not above hyping a book for a friend, this assuredly is not the case with *Prepare Your Church for the Future*.

Let me describe the significance of this book with carefully chosen words. As many know, I am a professional church-growth scholar, and I am familiar with what has been and is being done in the field. I myself have made several modest, but recognized contributions. I say all that to say this: *Prepare Your Church for the Future* may well be the most significant step forward in church growth theory and practice since Donald McGavran wrote the basic textbook, *Understanding Church Growth,* in 1970.

Carl George is in the top echelon of church growth analysts and consultants in the USA. For well over a decade he has immersed himself personally in the affairs of hundreds of churches affiliated with dozens of denominations. His main objective has been to understand himself and then help church leaders understand why their churches or denominations either grow or fail to grow. His passion is reaching the lost for Jesus Christ.

Prepare Your Church for the Future is a blueprint for unlimited growth. By studying the dynamics of the world's Meta-Churches numbering in the tens of thousands, Carl George has come up with a kind of do-it-yourself manual. The book is exquisitely how-to. I almost hate to say it, but it is about as thorough as a modern operator's manual for a new lap-top computer. But happily it's written in plain English and in a captivating literary style. Everything you need to know to understand and begin to apply Meta-Church theory is here.

Times change. Our society is on one of the steepest curves of technological, demographic, and psychological transformation imaginable. How can the church keep abreast? How can our methodology fit our modernity? Carl George shows us how.

What do you do with a book that says, "One day soon, North American churches of 25,000 to 50,000 will appear in every metropolitan area"? You read it to find out if the author can deliver the goods.

Read this one. You'll find out that he does!

C. PETER WAGNER
Fuller Seminary
Pasadena, California

SECTION I

Threshold of Opportunity

1
Prepare for Future Shock

I grew up near a small Mom-and-Pop store. "Pop" typically hovered around the hardware section, tinkering with fasteners he sold for two cents apiece but that, considering overhead costs, should have sold for twenty-five cents. Pop liked his puttering because he could get to know the customers. His relationship building helped patrons feel good about their visit, and it ensured that they'd come again.

"Mom" focused her energies in the well-organized housewares department. By featuring attractive, fashionable items, her profits more than compensated for the money lost on the underpriced fasteners.

Mom and Pop lacked the business vocabulary to articulate ideas like pinpointing their center of growth (housewares), capitalizing on their strengths (Pop's problem-solving ability and Mom's eye for newer lines), and reinforcing the reasons they initially opened the store (serving customers and maximizing profits so as to support the family).

To Mom and Pop, running the store had become a way of life. The daily rituals—sweeping the sidewalk and straightening the merchandise—in themselves provided a sense of security and comfort.

One day Mom and Pop realized that the needs of their customers had been changing. Lately some had indicated that getting in and out of a store quickly was more important than chatting with the proprietor. Others didn't want to buy merchandise unless they could choose from at least three different manufacturers. As a result, the people whom Mom and Pop wanted to serve were going elsewhere.

Mom and Pop sensed this dissonance and interpreted it as an ultimatum for change. They decided that to survive, Pop would install self-service hardware and Mom would take special orders. They once again placed higher priority on meeting customers' needs and maximizing profits than on maintaining the way of life they'd known and cherished.

In making these choices, Mom and Pop demonstrated how an organization can refocus its sights on the original impetus for its success. Recapturing that purpose is worth an interruption to familiar routines!

Churches* are faced with a similar dilemma. We quickly forget that the felt needs of our "customers" are in a constant state of flux. We can overlook the fact that each new day ushers in a slightly different set of circumstances. We sometimes neglect the long-range implications of not keeping abreast with the present. Instead, we often persevere in the comfortable habits to which we've grown accustomed.

What does our life-style say about our openness to change? Are we willing to face the reality that people, even spiritually hungry individuals, are passing us by as they walk down the street of life? Are we inclined to ask why, knowing that our blind spots might figure into the explanation?

We need to take a fresh look at what God has called us to be. We need a way of measuring our health and effectiveness. And we need a readiness to induce changes that are needed.

I believe that the choices challenging Christians today are so great that, for many local churches, their very existence is, or will soon be, at stake.

Fortunately, many men and women in leadership aren't ignoring the future. Evangelical researchers are pinpointing the significant trends of the 1990s and are discovering new biblical models being used of God

---

* Throughout this book, I'll use the word *church* to indicate a local body of believers (Pleasantville Community Church) or the sum of all churches (the church as the Body of Christ). The word *church* always refers to people, not their place of worship (which I term *church building* or *church facility*).

The word *congregation* will signify a certain-sized group (all the adults meet as a congregation before going into their Sunday-school classes). Therefore it's not a synonym for *church*. I'll comment further on this distinction in Chapter 4.

to seize the opportunities of our day. Churches are acknowledging that for our own spiritual health—much less survival—we must change.

Eight Needs

Where is our society headed? What will the future in which North American churches must minister be like? What will the typical person's felt needs be? Consider these glimpses offered by leading analysts of our era.

"I Still Value a Personal Touch"

John Naisbitt's 1982 best-seller *Megatrends*[1] proved to be a surprisingly accurate forecast. Now his *Megatrends 2000*[2] offers another equally fascinating set of predictions.

One trend described in both books indicates that with each new wave of technological advancements, people seek a compensatory human touch. For example, despite an explosion in sales of high-tech VCRs, human beings still need the "high-touch" experience of going to a movie theater with their friends. Even though airline computers daily juggle hundreds of air-traffic schedules, along with thousands of seating options, every major carrier has set up a telephone-reservation system that affords the personal touch of speaking with a human being about a specific flight and a particular seat.

The implication for churches? I believe that opportunities for interpersonal exchange, such as small caring groups, are needed more than ever.

"I Want Continual Options"

Men, women, teens, and children are coming to expect multiple-option choices in every area of their lives, according to Lyle Schaller, dean of American church observers, in *It's a Different World*.[3]

In a world that allows consumers to decide between not just three television networks, but up to two hundred channels, churches can no longer be designed with only one program option. Believers today want many scheduling choices available, from which they can select the one that best suits their circumstances.

"Help Me Know How to Filter the Nineties"

David McKenna, president of Asbury Seminary, in Kentucky, writes in *Mega Truth*[4] that the church must do two things as our society, believers and unbelievers alike, enters the Information Age.

First, Christians should face the fact that our world—including the makeup of North American churches—is in a process of dramatic change. Ninety percent of the jobs being created in the United States are in information industries, knowledge work, or other white-collar professions. The blue-collar sector presently represents less than two out of ten American workers, and that ratio continues to edge downward.

Second, church leaders must remember that the Information Age brings with it a set of values and priorities, just as does every other "ism" and trend. Thus, in the sorting-out process of how churches must therefore grow and adapt, we must keep our Bibles open. We must search for scriptural filters suitable to evaluate and respond to the presuppositions embodied in Western culture of the nineties.

"Enable Me to Cope With Change"

How do churchgoers and pastors feel about the way life today constantly demands that we adjust our framework of expectations and rules of thumb? Do we like this fact of living? Which thought patterns and work habits most affect our ability to deal with change? Futurist Joel Barker, in *Discovering the Future,*[5] emphasizes the need to develop a positive attitude toward inevitable rapid change.

Why isn't previous experience adequate for guiding a church leader into the future? In years past, for example, a minister could use shame and guilt to motivate members to participate in parish activities. Previously, even peripheral church attenders had the assumption that they "should" support the ministries of their fellowship. Or in Sundays gone by pastors could expect the faithful to sit contentedly through a forty-five-minute theological lecture, whether or not it related to day-to-day life.

Nowadays when people come to church activities, they expect their problems to be addressed. Their marriages, jobs, and relationships are unstable and falling apart. They're willing to get involved in church, but only if doing so will help answer their personal cries for help.

The rate of change in our society has become more intense than in any previous generation. These circumstances are creating a proliferation of ministry opportunities. If, however, we can't cope with change, our ability to influence others will diminish.

"Don't Overlook Any Women"

Among the ten world trends highlighted by Howard Snyder in *Foresight,*[6] one of the most notable deals with how men and women relate to one another.

The significance goes beyond the obvious social change of male domination in organizational leadership being replaced by a partnership of men and women. A fundamental shift of emphasis is occurring, says Snyder; the doing of ministry now receives more importance than the title of the doer.

Florence Nightingale's priority was the people who were dying because they weren't being cared for, yet the whole male-dominated British nursing system changed as a result. Likewise women today are transforming churches as they minister wherever they find spiritual sickness and no one else to help.

In times past, ministry has been focused on a title, a role, or a job description, and the person sought out was typically "the best man for the job." Now more importance is paid to the need for ministry, which can be done by anyone from the community of ministers known as the church.

"Capitalize on What Motivates Me"

Peter Drucker, noted writer on management science, observes in *The Age of Discontinuity*[7] that our era of rapid change is forcing business planners and managers to be more responsive to people's felt needs. His book *The New Realities*[8] includes a section that applies management principles to religious organizations. He observes that thriving churches are ones that have discovered creative ways to address a multiplicity of human interests.

All church leaders could profit by likewise asking themselves, *How would a marketing expert describe the fundamental motivations of the people of our parish?* The answer should then be used to shape each congregation's ministry and structure. The result will be more effective and widespread ministry.

"Show Me an Organizational Structure Where People Matter"

If the mission of many businesses (and of all churches) involves helping human lives be transformed, then what form and structure can best help that mission to be accomplished? Henry Mintzberg, a professor of management science, predicts in *Structure in Fives: Designing Effective Organizations*[9] that businesses will begin developing a "missionary organization" model for achieving their business goals.

Couldn't churches benefit from doing the same kind of self-examination of their structures? Are we geared more toward processing people or to the somewhat people-indifferent tasks of protecting our status quo and our pastor's job security? Does the typical local parish have more machinery in place to provide help for a newcomer with a troubled marriage or to perpetuate its existing activities?

"Show Me People Who Care"

In summer a beach contains both those who can't wait for the thrill of surfing and those who don't even like the waves. With this world becoming more turbulent all the time, says Tom Peters, in *Thriving on Chaos,*[10] organizations must empower each individual to embrace change. How? By treating each well and by being responsive to the customer's desire to know that the leadership cares.

Wal-Mart's, for instance, now employs customer greeters who smile and welcome each person entering the store with, "Hi! Nice to have you in today. Anything I can direct you to?" Or the shopping chain Nordstrom instructs its employees to see that the customer is satisfied, period. How can a corporation afford to do that? Peters notes that Nordstrom's profitability at that time exceeded all other soft-goods chains.

Similarly, the growth of the largest church in Christendom (in Seoul, Korea) stems from every tenth member being officially commissioned as a caregiver. Certainly, all members are taught to care for one another, but this system makes sure no one seeking help gets overlooked.

What if every church took this high-energy attitude toward mobilizing care giving, especially toward newcomers? Not only would a "new" biblical model of ministry emerge, but there would be a ready response in any group of people it targets.

Four Predictions

With all these changes afoot in the way the business world seeks to meet people's needs, inevitably questions will be raised about the effectiveness of the average church. A dangerous gap seems to be widening between the "service" promised by the community of God and what we actually provide, at least compared to what intelligent laypeople are currently leading their industries to do.

Ultimately, whether or not a church demonstrates the care and love of Christ boils down to its vision and structure. Know what you believe God wants you to do, develop the organizational framework so it can happen, and some amazing things will result. That's how the business community operates. If they can do it, why aren't we? We have God, and they have the dollar; surely God is a more durable and compelling motivation than the dollar!

What kind of vision will need to dominate the church of the future? What will its structure be? Can it actually accomplish Christ's Great Command (Matthew 22:37–40) and Great Commission (Matthew 28:18–20)? Here are four predictions.

1. We'll Plan for an Extended Future. I grew up with a keen awareness of living in the end times, in which Christ could return at any moment. This perspective motivated me to be ready and to pour my energies into things that will count for eternity.

Unfortunately, I allowed my "terminal generation" panic and zeal to keep me from visualizing an even bigger picture. I'm sorry that twenty years ago I didn't ask myself, *Suppose God decides to wait twenty more years? What kind of planning should I do?*

Today I'm still ready—and eager—for Christ's second coming. But I'm also asking, *What if God delays two hundred years? What if, when we hit the year 2000, we're only at the halfway point of the church age, with two thousand more years to come? What kind of responses should I have made?*

Suppose God has planned an extended future for the church? If so, our ministry dreams should receive the kind of planning appropriate to building a European cathedral rather than the all-too-common approach of throwing on another tar-paper patch that may last a whopping two or three years! When I meet the Lord, I don't want Him to ask, "Carl George, why did you check out so early?"

2. Urban Area Churches Will Set the Pace. Our generation will experience the most massive increase in human population since the beginning of time. In the process, metro-area churches will become increasingly important.

Our opportunities are greater today than at any other time in human history. As world population continues to explode, life on earth will increasingly become metropolitan. The number of world-class cities (those with a population greater than 5 million) has mushroomed from 7 in 1950, to 34 in 1984. By the year 2025, the total will reach 93.[11]

The implications are staggering. Already 50 percent of the world's people live in cities (up from 33 percent in 1970).[12] From now on, at least seven out of every eight people born will spend their whole lives as part of an urban sprawl.[13] If these people are to have church homes, the vast majority of the world's churches will be found in metropolitan areas. (*See* Chart 1.)

Will United States and Canadian urban centers be pacesetters for the world of the future? Probably not. Almost all the urbanization will occur not in industrialized nations, but in developing regions known as the Third World. For example, eighty of the ninety-three world-class cities will be in emerging countries.[14]

Not only, then, will the typical church of the future be in the suburban shadow of some world-class city, but the people of that assembly will be nonwhite. I predict that churches of today represent the final generation of Western dominance in Christendom.

In short, if Christ's Great Commission is to be fulfilled, future churches must be where the people are:

Most growth through A.D. 2025 will be in metropolitan areas.
Most growth through A.D. 2025 will be in Third World countries.
These urban centers will have populations greater than 5 million:
1950 = 7 (New York, London, Paris, Rhein-Ruhr, Tokyo-Yokohama, Shanghai, Buenos Aires)

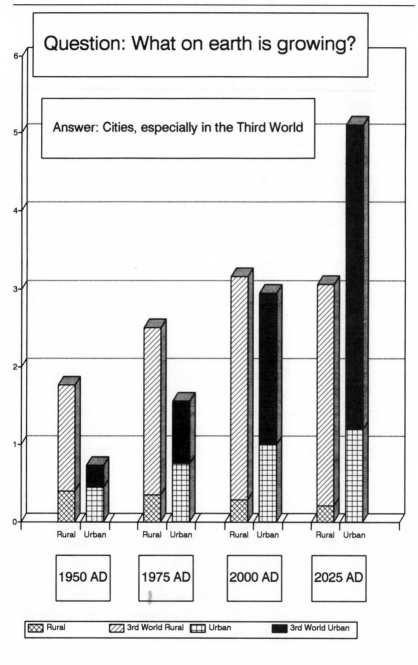

Chart 1

1984 = 34 cities

2025 = 93 cities, 80 of which will be in emerging countries[15]

3. Smaller Churches Will Have Part-time Pastors. By the time we cross the year 2000, most smaller churches will be pastored by volunteers and "tentmakers" (the Apostle Paul's source of income in Acts 18:1–3; 20:34 and elsewhere). These pastors of the future will be equipped with a system of ministry to be described later in this book.

Their new set of tools will make them capable, as self-supporting bivocational clergy, of more effective ministry to larger numbers of people than is now achieved by full-time pastors working under current ministry models!

4. Huge Churches Will Be Small Enough to Care. I predict that many churches of the future will be larger than anything we've imagined. In fact, the next generation of churches will dwarf our current successes—including the world's largest, the great congregation in Seoul, which is rapidly pushing toward a three-quarters of a million figure!

Churches, though large, will be more personal than ever. A recent radio advertisement for the huge Wells Fargo Bank announced a twenty-four-hour phone service, which it took pains to point out, wasn't answered by computer or recording, but by one very real person. This corporate model affirms the possibility for churches to reach the same goal: keep growing bigger while organizing the "consumers" into ever-smaller groupings so they can be cared for in even more personal ways.

For example, the Yoido Full Gospel Church, in Seoul, Korea, had more than 650,000 participants at the end of the 1980s, up from 100,000 a decade earlier. Yet as the size increased, the "care delivery system" became smaller and more personalized. From most members' perspective, their church fellowship rarely appears to be larger than ten or twenty people. These are called home cells and are led by some 55,000 home-group leaders. This system enables each of 650,000 individuals to receive individual spiritual attention.

Thus the church of the future, though far bigger than the typical parish of today, will not be known for its central meeting spot, but for its small-group-ministry "franchise." In the business community, a franchiser like McDonald's provides know-how and product recognition, while the local franchisee supplies the local contact with customers. The franchiser empowers the local group as an authorized provider of desirable products and services.

I believe pastors and church leadership will adopt a franchiser attitude toward their member-ministers in each section of a town. Members will be encouraged to set up neighborhood outlets, such as home-cell groups, throughout their church's "service area." They will be empowered through training from their church's leadership.

It is my contention in this book that our present models for doing ministry are ineffective and inadequate for the opportunities that are coming our way. If Christian churches are to receive the harvest of souls that we believe God is calling to enter His kingdom, it will happen only because churches have reorganized their structures. They must be large enough to make a difference and yet small enough to care. As Frank Tillapaugh has said so well, it's time to unleash the church![16]

Who Can Survive?

My dad was born in the year 1900. He and I often laugh at the world of social changes he's lived through. We joke that in his day fast foods were what people ate during Lent, outer space was the back of the Riviera Drive-In Theater, designer jeans were scheming girls named *Jean,* having a meaningful relationship meant getting along well with one's cousins, a chip was a piece of wood, hardware meant nuts and bolts, and software was a T-shirt!

After talking with him one night, I listed the series of technological exploits he's witnessed during his lifetime:

What's New Since 1900?

A   Airplanes, air conditioners, animated cartoons, AIDS

B   Bullet trains, bamboo-curtain's falling, birth control

C   Computers, cholesterol awareness, chemical warfare

D   Deep-sea exploration, drug cartels, dual-career couples

E   Environmentalism, extended life span, electronic music

F   Fall of the iron curtain, FAX machines, fast foods, fiber optics

G   Gene splicing, global warming, guerrilla warfare, gas engines

H   High-speed external elevators, home-delivered pizza, helicopters

I   International money markets, Israel in Palestine, immigration

J   Jet airplanes, Japan as economic superpower, jeans

K   Kremlin peristroika, kidney transplants, Kuwait's occupation, killer bees

L   Liberation movement for minorities and women, legal abortion

M   Megacities, molecular biology, microwave ovens, Mars landing

N   Nuclear bombs and power, national debt, Neptune moon photos

O   Oil shortages, overfishing of the seas, ozone warnings

P   Pentecostal renewal, plastic credit cards, pornography

Q   Quick credit, quotas in workplace, quarks, quantum theory

R   Robots, rock music, rain-forest destruction, radar

S   Space travel, spy satellites, subways, satanism, skyjacking

T   Transplant surgery, television, terrorism, toxic wastes

U   Unreached-peoples awareness, unions, uterus microsurgery

V   Video cassette recorders, Volkswagens, Vietnam War

W   Wonder drugs, World Wars, wind farming, women in workplace, war and politics

X   Xerox photocopying, X rays and chemotherapy

Y   Yalta Conference and German unification, yoga, yen currency

Z   Zero-gravity manufacturing, Zeppelin flight and crash

Just after my dad turned ninety, I asked him how he's managed to adapt to the bewildering blur of changes that he's had to live through. ''That's easy,'' he said. ''Just remember that it's terribly important not to hang around 'old' people!''

May the church seize that same perspective! Far more seriously, may we also realize that we *must* respond to our era of unparalleled change and opportunity. Our very survival may depend on it.

2
Tally What You Inherited

Your church didn't just happen. If you investigate carefully, you'll discover a number of specific strategies, which from a human perspective, produced the growth evident in your church today. You may think of your church as an avant-garde independent congregation with no heritage. Or maybe it's a tradition-saturated denominational shrine that hasn't adopted an innovative idea for the last two hundred years! Whatever the case, your church embodies growth sources that can be both identified and analyzed.

If you can understand the patterns by which present-day churches have developed into their current sizes and structures, you'll be able to evaluate certain factors that have influenced your own church (Chapter 3) and to see the wisdom of synthesizing a new model for growth (Chapters 4 and 5).

This chapter offers a tour of sixteen methodologies that most church leaders have either observed or experienced. As you review them, notice how each was perceived largely as a program having an assumed organization; that is, the issue of how to organize the vision was often treated as inseparable from the program itself.

Thus the frequently present smaller-size group or intermediate-size group within the whole has seemed unimportant. Group sizes in most of these examples are often perceived as auxiliary, incidental, or over-looked.

What kind of increased spiritual and numerical results might have occurred if the organization of these subgroups had been more intentionally studied and cultivated? As you read, ask yourself that question (we'll focus on groups in Chapters 6 through 9). A central premise of this book is that a pastor should elevate to first priority the promotion and multiplication of certain smaller groups; they are the essential centers of growth.

Preaching and Revivals

The makeshift pulpits of itinerate evangelists and revivalist ministers shaped this continent's frontier era as powerfully as Christ's apostles transformed the spiritual face of the Roman Empire. Fervent preaching and demonstrations of spiritual power stimulated conversions and church growth and resulted in the founding of numerous denominations.

In the southern United States, early Baptist churches flourished with little reliance on Sunday-school methodology or pastoral training; firebrand preaching made the difference. Likewise, in the eastern region of America, the Methodist and Presbyterian Awakening of the early nineteenth century sparked impassioned preaching and evidences of spiritual conviction everywhere, from respected universities to frontier camp meetings.

Pulpiteers like Jonathan Edwards, George Whitefield, Samuel Davies, Lyman Beecher, James McGready, Peter Cartwright, Francis Asbury, Daniel Marshall, Charles Finney, Catherine Booth, and dozens of others were household names. People like ex-baseball player Billy Sunday, who would tear apart a chair on stage as if striking the devil, made preaching such a sensational event that it drew newspaper coverage.

Each of these colorful personalities demonstrated a willingness to do the unusual in order that the gospel might be proclaimed. These orators believed passionately in the power of enthusiastic preaching. As evangelist D. L. Moody, who proclaimed the gospel to an estimated 100 million people during his life, said, "The best way to revive the church is to build a fire in the pulpit."[1]

Sunday School

Sunday schools have contributed to church growth by going beyond what the pulpit could do. With their emphasis on lay involvement, they quickly became one of the most widely used methods to organize support for an embryo parish.

Although the Sunday school was born in England as a social ministry to teach poor children to read, North Americans used it more as an outreach tool. Under the leadership of lay teachers, an outpost Sunday school would gradually solidify into a preaching point for adults as well. This would grow into an organized church. Eventually the people would bring in a paid, "real" pastor.

Seminaries, from the colonial era to the present, haven't significantly prepared the typical pastor for working with the dynamics of a lay-led program like the Sunday school. Thus, often without much knowledgeable guidance from a minister, the Sunday-school movement has provided meaningful roles for active lay ministry. Maybe this circumstance was a plus: It freed a church to go beyond the limitations of its pastor's vision and ability. It gave laypeople a chance to make growth happen.

Consider, for example, this illustration from a detailed account of a Sunday-school campaign that occurred in the 1920s. In those days demographic statistics were not readily available, so skilled Sunday-school organizers would canvass a community to note the residence of every unchurched child in the region. These laymen and -women would tabulate their survey findings by ages: "We found 25 six-year-olds, 34 seven-year-olds," and so on.

Next they'd go into the church's adult Bible classes and present the challenge in specific terms: "We need three teachers for six-year-olds, four teachers for seven-year-olds," and so on.

Inspired by concrete goals, the new teaching recruits would accept names for their responsibility lists, begin a six-week visitation campaign, and literally triple the size of the Sunday school! When the organizing personnel moved on, attendance would sag by as much as a third. But the net result was still a doubled Sunday-school membership!

This experience was repeated enough times that millions of people entered church life for the first time through the Sunday school, with the human credit going to laypeople who had accepted meaningful leadership roles within their churches.

The most prolific North American Protestant group, the Southern Baptists, credits its growth not only to divinely empowered preaching built on sound evangelistic theology, but also to its system of Sunday-school organization that gives laypeople a very significant role as lay ministers.

The basic idea, called the Flake Formula (named after a Christian-education person in the 1940s), is that each trained and commissioned Sunday-school teacher will increase attendance by about ten people. Similarly the ten-by-one rule says that a volunteer lay class leader can best handle a group of about ten people.

Even with the limitation of being "required" to meet on church premises (no church roof over a ministry too often means no church vision for it), the Sunday school has been for two centuries a lay-led, small-group movement highly effective in producing church growth.

Bus Ministry

Bus ministry, popularized in the 1960s, was a breakthrough tactic used by many churches to stimulate large numerical growth. In the process it led to a major change in how Sunday school was implemented.

Before busing came to be, a children's Sunday-school teacher would be the sole shepherd of about ten children. He or she served as caller and recruiter, through home visits, phone calls, and postcard reminders. On Sunday, after some department-wide singing and announcements, this person would gather the ten children, meet with them in a little room, try to hold their attention, and teach them!

Bus ministry changed that equation by separating the recruiting functions from the teaching functions. One team spent Saturday inviting the youngsters and Sunday transporting them, plus conducting activities en route, from Scripture memory to prize giveaways. A second group was waiting to receive this ready-made audience. Their responsibility was to hold their attention, maintain order, and motivate learning.

A case in point is First Baptist Church, Hammond, Indiana, which, under the leadership of Pastor Jack Hyles, became the largest Sunday school in North America. At the time I visited, there were six shifts of Sunday schools, fed by a fleet of some two hundred buses!

The chief mechanic was a huge man who could almost intimidate a bus into starting: He'd bark orders at the driver, yank on the wiring, and zap the bus with an electrical charging device. Rather than taking abuse, he—typical of Hammond culture—knew how to give it! (What a far cry from the Florida university-town church I served, where our bus program was staffed by Ph.D.s who found bus wrestling most distasteful!)

The vehicles soon returned full of kids. These weren't typical suburban tykes; they were the sort tough steel-mill workers could round up and wrangle into obedience. The workers didn't disperse the children ten at a time to little old ladies to be taught; some of these kids were the kind who would snatch purses and slash tires!

Instead, the bus captains poured the youngsters, several hundred at a time, into large rooms that had big, burly bus drivers stationed around the wall and at every table. Discipline was maintained by something even the rascals respected: a muscular arm on the shoulder, connected to a deep voice that said, "Sit down, kid." This was, unfortunately, more attention and love than many of them received at home.

In the front of the room, teams of master teachers held the children's attention better than many a pulpit minister could. They were capable people, many of them women with years of experience teaching public school. They skillfully used a microphone, puppet stage, and a variety of other teaching aids.

Even the building architecture for this Sunday school was different from the typical cubbyhole cluster of rooms in the basement of an educational wing. At First Baptist, Hammond, everything was large— rooms, hallways, and juice dispensers!

Did bus programs succeed everywhere? Only if the social match was right. Many of the bused children were the neglected latchkey sort from unchurched working-class homes. If a church's bus workers and the children's families were on the same social level, that church could effectively reach the parents as well. If not, use of buses tended to be phased out.

Did bus ministry, with its new system of groups and organization, lead to larger churches? Yes. Most churches that were first to cross the 1,000 attendance threshold in the sixties and seventies used busing to achieve that breakthrough.

Feeder and Receptor Patterns

Why do some churches grow even without being strongly evangelistic? The most common explanation, which fits many of the large metropolitan-area churches, is that some develop a gravitational pull on the unhappy, the disillusioned, and the underutilized from other churches.

I first learned of this phenomenon in publications from the Church of the Nazarene. They observed it in areas with a number of little churches from a similar tradition. Whenever members responded to internal congregational troubles by looking elsewhere for a new church home, they tended to drift to one or more churches that had distinguished themselves as receptor sites. These would grow large as a result of recurring troubles in the feeder churches. (*See* Illustration 1.)

At least five feeder-to-receptor pathways can be identified. The first involves moral failure. Perhaps the youth minister and a choir member get involved in a tryst, and the unholy relationship breaks open in an ugly public scene. Several families with teenagers may respond with, "We must protect our children from this poor modeling; let's get out." So they look for somewhere that seems more stable—a bigger church.

Second, a key man or woman may intimidate the small-church pastor and consequently decide to leave. Maybe the person is gifted as a persuasive communicator, highly educated, or more socially popular than the minister. Either the pastor feels threatened or the high-ability layperson feels shunned. So the lay leader and family opt to find a bigger church, where they can be less conspicuous and less intimidating—or where there's a pastor with a higher ability level or is more secure.

Third, fast-track individuals with large incomes from professional and business success frequently find that their riches place them in an increasingly hostile environment within their small church. A busi-

Mega-Church Formation

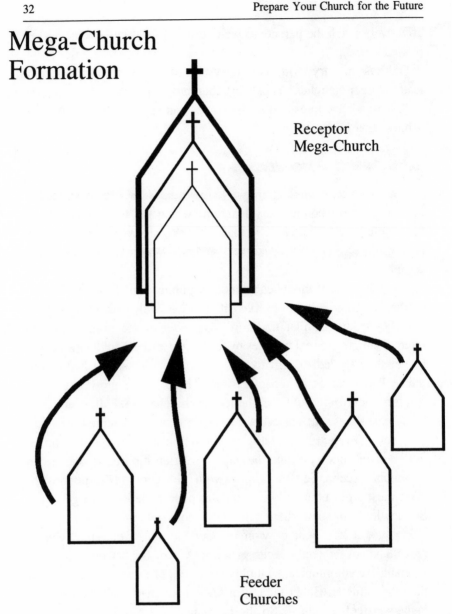

Receptor
Mega-Church

Feeder
Churches

Illustration 1

nessperson who employs other people, for example, will feel awkward in disciplining workers on the job and then attending church with them on Sunday.

Or due to the higher-income factor, church people may begin to make snide remarks about the entrepreneur's nicer clothes, more expensive recreation, bigger house, or newer car. Soon the family feels uncomfortable in their church and searches out a larger social berth.

An interesting twist on this third category is the divorced person. A single parent, who may have a lesser income, often feels snubbed by the smaller church. In search of approval and to escape the punishment of criticism, such an individual will gravitate toward the anonymity of one of the large receptor churches.

Fourth, even a healthy small church may be unable to meet the needs of all its families, particularly those with teens. Often the parents of junior- and senior-high young people find their children becoming reluctant to attend their home church and increasingly enamored with another church's strong teen program and attractive teenagers. Churches with a growing attendance above 400, for example, are almost always distinguished by flourishing youth ministry.

Finally, people with a high level of musical talent or cultivated taste may decide that their small church lacks opportunities for using their gifts or for providing the level of musical refinement that their culture requires. Musicians and artists frequently desire to join others with similar interests. Their search often leads them to the larger church.

Most Christians who graduate from a feeder church to a receptor church arrive a little burned out and somewhat irritated about the weaknesses of their previous church. Within a year, healing usually occurs. Many of the newcomers have good spiritual formation, basic Bible knowledge, and a developed commitment to tithing. Some may look for opportunities for ministry; others may vegetate for years.

Either way, they don't require much pastoral maintenance, because the minister's personal touch had little to do with why they came. All the new church has to do is be the least-worst choice of the searching family, and it will grow in size!

Intentional Positioning

A marketing term called *positioning* can be applied to churches that purposely restructure their image in order to be more appealing to the people they want to reach. Getting "positioned" does not always lead to largeness. It can, however, situate a fellowship so that it can grow through being a receptor church.

A church might intentionally target a certain group, such as upwardly mobile people. My own Baptist denomination, for example, had a heritage of poor, little-educated pastors working with poor, working-class people. Thus we've not been perceived by elite, sophisticated people as a crowd they'd like to join.

Over the years, however, as some Baptist laypeople became better educated or more prosperous in business, they'd change to a church where they felt more comfortable, often to an established, downtown "First Baptist Church." A difference, even a resentment, would develop between the rural or suburban churches and what they would call "those snooty blue bloods, with their fancy building downtown, at First Baptist."

These differences in churches provide space within the same denomination for upward social mobility. But where do rural-background Baptists of the second generation go for a step upward, if they're alienated from the downtown church by memories of their parents' negative comments? Some join a mainline denomination, the Methodists, Presbyterians, or Episcopalians. This latter group is positioned in an apex position, the last option short of Rome. As such it's a receptor church for many Protestants in search of a middle ground, such as couples who come from diverse denominational backgrounds and Protestant-Catholic marriages seeking a safe haven.

Some churches position themselves without meaning to. The church I pastored in Gainesville, Florida, for instance, was for a decade unlike anything else around. I was the only local pastor with parents from the Midwest, so we became the only nonsouthern-culture Baptist church in town. For anyone who had just moved south, we were the least-worst choice among a dozen churches of our doctrinal stripe.

Frankly, most receptor churches were not intentionally positioned. They just "happened," by God's grace, to hire the right staff member or launch the right ministry at the right time. This created a growth streak that led them ahead of the pack and made them be perceived as the church with momentum—the place to go! These churches stumbled on something that worked for them, so they kept doing it.

Apex positioning can occur intentionally as well. A church can deliberately set out to situate itself to become seen as the most viable option for meeting the spiritual and social needs of whatever segment of the population God's Spirit prompts it to target.

Music Center

Some churches function as music centers, wielding a powerful attraction on a segment of people who want certain musical experiences and opportunities. There may be a huge choir, a pipe organ, or a contemporary band with guitars and synthesizers. Whatever the variety of taste, these churches are places people enjoy attending for the music.

Many Pentecostal and charismatic churches trace much of their growth to enthusiastic, full-bodied praise, usually cued by music. It's no coincidence that most religious radio and television shows are produced by the Pentecostals and charismatics. They know from experience that sooner or later many of their listeners will check out the churches that feature such sounds.

A dramatic illustration of the preevangelistism impact of religious media occurred in the late 1980s, when scandals toppled several prominent television evangelists. Many Pentecostal and Assemblies of God churches found that their visitor flow practically dried up overnight. Their preevangelism media communication system had suddenly become a channel for bad news, and it noticeably hampered visitor flow for at least a year.

This same attraction phenomenon applies in churches characterized by the more elegant forms of music. They are known for their organ and choral quality, and they become classical-music centers.

Church size, predictably, will relate to the size of the population segment that's drawn to the musical taste represented in that particular church.

Pulpit Teaching and Oratory Skills

Preaching in more recent times is a far cry from the fiery sermonizing of previous centuries. Today's eloquent speaking represents a level of erudition and refinement that couldn't have meshed with the social context of the frontier era.

Contemporary pastors are exceptional teachers, capable of conveying imaginative word pictures. They hang images in a person's mind, much as paintings adorn the walls of an art gallery.

Today's sermons stem from a communication style that's both conversational and flawlessly clear. Well-known pastors like John MacArthur, Charles Swindoll, Ben Hayden, Gordon MacDonald, and Lloyd Ogilvie speak with such polish that they could be published with little editing.

Robert H. Schuller, in fact, sometimes compiles his sermons in book form before he preaches them. In one of his telecasts, he quoted one of his own newly published books, explaining, "There is something I want to say about that, right here." So we heard Schuller read Schuller!

No one would liken the style of these dynamic speakers to the impassioned and colorful antics of the Billy Sundays of yesteryear, nor would audiences respond to them in the same ways bygone audiences responded in the spiritual revivals that once swept across the continent. These contemporary pulpiteers are nevertheless master communicators who draw huge followings. Their powerful preaching is a major reason for their ever-enlarging attendances.

Miracle Ministry

Interest in divine healing touches every social class of sickly people. For years I looked dubiously on such miracle ministries. Then, in late 1983, I learned that I had cancer. "You see this mass?" the doctor bluntly asked me as he showed me my X rays. "That is why I am scheduling you for surgery this Thursday."

Various circumstances delayed the operation for six weeks. During this time I gained a whole new understanding about how people are motivated! No miracle evangelist was beneath my notice. No broadcasts, not the slickest series on how to make a million dollars through real estate, could hold my interest like the unschooled Pentecostal who faced the camera and spoke of God's healing. I even sought prayer for my illness at special services led by a faith healer who was touring nearby Presbyterian churches.

The morning before my surgery I asked the nurse for one last sonogram, explaining, "I have people praying for me."

"I'm a Christian," she replied. "So I know where you're coming from."

Unfortunately the test revealed no changes. I thank God the doctor was able to remove all the cancer. He termed it luck, but I called it a blessing of God that I was healed.

I know the Lord sometimes removes human infirmity without the help of doctors. I also acknowledge His use of modern medicine. But most of all I've learned that when someone is under the threat of mortal illness, even a highly rational personality like my own will seriously investigate any church or group of Christians that focuses on healing. It's no longer a wonder to me that crowds gather for such ministry.

Capture by Committee Involvement

Some denominations, like the Presbyterians, Lutherans, and Episcopalians, have become captive to the upper middle class. How does a church keep these often materialistic, high-power people interested and involved? One solution is to offer them a seat on the church board, or after that's filled, to place them on a significant committee, giving, them veto-making authority in order to meet their power needs. In some smaller churches, up to half the adult membership is involved in one of these groups.

Sadly, once it has filled the available slots, this system only guarantees that little or nothing can be approved. It resembles a passenger train's brake cord that any passenger can pull at any time from any car, forcing the entire locomotive to a screeching halt. There is only one accelerator, and it's located in the front of the train. But access to it was lost when the church founders passed away. So in most cases a multitude of boards and committees serve mainly to prevent new vision from taking the church beyond the status quo.

Day Schools

The Christian day-school strategy works well in places where parents have a general antigovernment bias or where the public schools are viewed as spiritually unsafe or academically substandard. Sometimes this alternative education system may deter parents from moving out of a changing neighborhood in which the public schools are deteriorating. This doesn't always produce growth, but it at least reduces the rate families exit the church. In rare cases, not only are Christian day schools and nursery day-care centers a potent growth strategy, they're also effective fund raisers for the church. Church-run preschools can be growth stimulators. But Christian day schools, with all their facility and administrative needs, tend to cause more problems than expansion.

Next-Door-to-the-Right-Institution Syndrome

Many churches profit from an in-town denominational feeder system such as a college, medical center, orphanage, retirement home, or denominational headquarters. These employ or train ready-made parishioners who need little incentive to fellowship within their church tradition and among friends from work or school.

Thus it's not so much this particular church's strengths that have recruited them as other career-shaping forces and prior loyalties.

High-Visibility and High-Profile Guests

Churches, particularly charismatic ones, create incredible momentum with publicity like, "Carman will be here next week! Last week he was in Dallas! Maybe you saw his Chicago concert recently on our local Christian TV station!"

Such local churches resemble talent showcases. Through wide broadcast promotion, even communitywide direct-mail blitzes, a local church can serve as a whistle-stop on a nationwide circuit, a contemporary Chautauqua that brings cutting-edge leaders to a host of locations.

Appealing, Mixed-Media Seeker Services

Some churches are experimenting with a worship-service format that mixes relevant preaching with a variety of performing ensembles and multimedia entertainment.

The most visible example is Willow Creek Community Church, located in the Chicago suburb of Barrington, Illinois. Under the leadership of founding pastor Bill Hybels, its 15,000-plus attenders have become the United States' second-largest church.

The Saturday-night and Sunday-morning services are a high-quality dramatic production. The targeted audience—unchurched baby boomers—are entertained, educated, and enlightened through interpretative movement, verse choir, reader's theater, dramatic ensemble, or even a well-played classical piano. The pastor speaks to contemporary issues in plain language. Visitors can see something more interesting than the Johnny Carson show, while at the same time, without being scolded or condemned for being unchurched pagans, they learn how to take some next steps toward God and toward a biblical way of life.

Hybels terms this strategy "seeker services" (or more accurately, seeker-friendly services, where believers can bring friends). It enlists the entire membership into recruitment committees of one. They initiate friends with testimonials like this: "I went to church last week, and it was so different that it wasn't even like church. You've got to come and see this!"

Multiple Staff

As churches grow, they tend to hire an additional pastor for each 100 new people. In most multiple-staff arrangements, only one or two of the ministers have a responsibility for systematically promoting growth through outreach and lay ministry. The rest have programmatic, administrative, office-bound positions.

A few churches require all staff to be in the field—and with very favorable results. For example, during the 1950s, a growing church in Cincinnati, the Landmark Baptist Temple, combined multiple staff and bus ministry with much success. I was present on the day of their highest attendance rally to date, celebrated by "Feeding the 5,000," in which they served 5,000 fish sandwiches, prepared by a local fast-food chain.

The staff did an enormous amount of contact work, each being expected to make as many as 500 contacts a week. The pastors accomplished these quotas by both phone and carefully mapped home visitations.

The vitality of this growth strategy was not in the visitation pastors' pushing themselves hard, but in the way the entire staff focused on making personal evangelistic contacts.

Immigration and Colonization

The history of North American Christianity is rich with accounts of new immigrants sending a call back to their motherland for a pastor or priest of their particular tradition. That's why in the Deep South, near a munitions plant that originally hired German engineers, one can find a Lutheran church. The concept also explains how Jack Hyles's large southern-culture Baptist church can thrive in northern Indiana's Calumet steel region. Steel mills were in times past labor-hungry employment magnets that hired workers from the Ozarks and the hills of Tennessee. Hyles came a generation later, but the immigrant population was still awaiting someone who understood their needs and fears and could effectively facilitate spiritual growth within their culture.

From Italians in Queens, New York, to Scandinavians in Minnesota, ethnic migration accounts for many large, or once-large, churches.

Subcongregations of Adults

At Lake Avenue Congregational, Peter Wagner leads the "120 Fellowship," a large class that has prayer ministry as its focus. It has helped many find healing power. One of the United States' larger Presbyterian churches is in Livonia, Michigan, under the leadership of Bartlett and Margaret Hess. In the church gymnasium 600 people gather each Sunday morning to sit captivated by a licensed Christian psychologist doing group therapy. Broken, hurting individuals attend the class for a couple of years until they're recovered enough to be involved with other groups in the church. On a weekday morning, another subcongregation draws several hundred for a women's ministry, led by the pastor's wife.

Such effective programs account for much growth in the churches that sponsor them.

The Future Goes Beyond the Classical Methods by Focusing on Small Groups. Clearly, God has used many strategies to build His church. Many parishes that grew large almost didn't mean to; the Holy Spirit placed in their path the right combination of talent and resources. Some seem to have grown almost by accident or the default of others. The issue of organizing for growth through developing leaders for small- and intermediate-sized subgroups has often been an after-thought.

The crucial nature of spiritual formation and how it is induced is not widely understood. Few church leaders seem to know which processes and structures should be intentionally cultivated in order to encourage the most significant growth streams.

I believe that the smaller group within the whole—called by dozens of terms, including the *small group* or the *cell group*—is a crucial but underdeveloped resource in most churches. It is, I contend, the most strategically significant foundation for spiritual formation and assimi-lation, for evangelism and leadership development, for the most essential functions that God has called for in the church.

The model for a healthy and thriving church, as outlined in future chapters, highlights the lay-led small group as the essential growth center. It's so important that everything else is to be considered secondary to its promotion and preservation.

3
Rattle the Cage Around Your Zoo

All churches, no matter what their size, must deal with a certain organizational issue if they're to experience the ongoing, quality growth that stems from Christ's Great Commission to "make disciples" (Matthew 28:18–20).

What's the crux of the difficulty? Pick the most likely answer:

1. Churches can't handle the high costs associated with buying more properties and constructing the additional buildings needed to spur organizational growth.
2. Churches can't attract new people because they can't compete with the quality of services, from day care for children to special jobs for people with handicaps, that corporations and governmental agencies now offer.
3. Churches don't have enough specialists, lay or pastoral, capable of handling the increasing load of federal and municipal red tape imposed on religious organizations.
4. Churches find that each time they grow a little, their quality

lessens, so they must scramble to implement a new organizational system geared to their current size.

The best answer is 4. This problem of organization has been around since the very first church in Jerusalem. True, it modeled an unusual depth of quality:

> They devoted themselves to the apostles' teaching and to the fellowship, to the breaking of bread and to prayer. Everyone was filled with awe, and many wonders and miraculous signs were done by the apostles. . . . Every day they continued to meet together. . . . And the Lord added to their number daily those who were being saved.
>
> Acts 2:42, 43, 46, 47

Very quickly, however, First Jerusalem Church's numerical expansion threatened to undo these strengths. It outgrew its ability to follow through on what it professed, and some of the widows, especially the Grecian-culture ones, who had returned from living abroad, began to be left hungry and feel that fellow believers didn't care about them.

In light of the young church's success, its quality could continue only if structural reorganization took place. The solution was to select seven wise, Spirit-filled men of Greek culture, with good contacts in the community, of those who had returned from living abroad, who would oversee food distribution, thus extending the distribution beyond what the twelve apostles could do, if they were to give attention to other dimensions of leadership. As a result, the church "increased rapidly" once more (*see* Acts 6:1–7).

Almost every growing church I've encountered faces insurmountable limits on its ability to expand its structure without serious disruption of quality. Sometimes the group thrives in spite of its organizational frustrations. The pastors are usually so tired, however, that if asked to visualize further growth, such as doubling or tripling, they respond with pain and despair. "If ministry will be harder if we become bigger," they say with physical and emotional fatigue, "then let's not do it."

Even more serious is the fact that, with very few exceptions, all significantly large churches in the United States and Canada are receptor churches built on a system of feeder churches, which I described in Chapter 2. In one situation I studied, it appeared that over 95 percent of the growth had come from other fellowships, rather than from new conversions.

How can you reorganize a church so that enlarged caring can occur without sacrificing quality? How can you restructure a ministry to catch up with and involve additional people who are already present? The vision of an ever-expanding, unsaved, unreached population seems to call for increasingly larger churches, as well as more churches of every size. What's the missing link?

This chapter will lead you on a tour of various-sized churches. Through this journey, you'll see the organizational frameworks that churches and subcongregations tend to use at different stages in their development. You'll be able to evaluate the limitations of each. You'll understand why there's a need for an organizational model that allows unlimited expansion without sacrificing quality growth.

That new paradigm, called the *Meta-Church*, will receive detailed explanation in subsequent chapters.

Mouse-Size Home Group

Beyond the family level, the most basic cluster of believers possible is a small, informal gathering. Such a conclave typically contains about ten people, although it may be as small as five or large as thirty-five. It's mouselike both in size and in the tendency to congregate in homes.

Known historically to many Christians in the United States as *cottage prayer meetings,* these asssemblies have been sponsored by churches since frontier days. The common perception is that these home extensions of a church are of a noncontinuous nature, as evidenced by the label *meetings* instead of *groups*. Such nomenclature speaks of events, not relationships.

Today's generation, starting with the Body Life movement of the 1970s, has placed much emphasis on the ten-person-or-so group. Much of the impetus originates from Christian literature houses and parachurch ministries, although an increasing number of churches make a plan for home groups in their programming.

Both historically and at present, relationship-based, small, home-based groups are usually perceived as an *elective* component of church life. Few clergy rely on them as the keystone of their growth strategy.

Cat-Size Small Church

The most frequently found church in the United States and Canada is the small fellowship. The Sunday-morning norm for half the churches in either of these countries is to have up to fifty people gathered for worship. If we include churches with an average attendance of seventy people or less, we've covered nearly 70 percent of North American Christianity's houses of worship.

In these churches, full-time professional pastoral leadership is optional. Ministers tend to be clients of people who meet together. If they have a pastor, it's nice; if not, it's almost as nice! They mainly need somebody to come by once in a while for sacraments and burials. The clergy must be a generalist who concentrates on leading worship and making obligatory visits.

Church analyst Lyle Schaller has termed these fellowships cat-size churches,[1] because they're independent; they behave toward their ministers the way cats behave toward their owners. A cat doesn't need its caregiver. It comes in for feeding once in a while, but it's durable enough to manage for itself.

A church with this characteristic will have a pastor for a while, get behind in finances, get rid of the pastor, catch up, and call another cleric. Pulpit vacancies seem to be part of the long-term budget-balancing strategy.

Cat-size churches are typically a clan, with the matriarchs and patriarchs being far more influential than the minister. The watchword when they gather is, "So nice to see you at worship again!" Most people in these assemblies come from just a few families, so worship is largely a public outcropping of their kinship network. Cat-size churches tend to function as one huge committee.

The cat-size church makes its decisions off the building premises, during their ongoing clan gatherings. Some of the fighting emerges in official congregational meetings, but most of the political work takes place elsewhere.

Thus, a cat-size church is hard to break into and difficult to change. Any one of its clannish guardians can blackball a newcomer or veto an idea.

It rarely grows beyond fifty, because its durable structure needs years for a new person to penetrate. God Himself doesn't presume to send new members without nine months' warning! With most of its growth being from biological sources, the cat-size church is preeminently a family church.

Lap-Dog-Size Medium Church

Churches with attendances of 100 or so will typically have one pastor and a number of lay-led organizations.

Certain unwritten rules teach that it's okay, even desirable, for the minister not to do certain things that "should" be the responsibility of the parishioners. Thus a number of volunteers will share in the ministry by heading up various groups, beginning with an age-graded Sunday school, but often also including a choir and a women's program. In each, one layperson tends to be in charge of about ten people.

These durable groups are hard to kill. Lay leaders take ownership of them, and pastors tend not to meddle. Other organizations will crop up as the church develops further.

I call this medium-size group a lap-dog-size church. It likes the companionship of a pastor and treats pastors very well. Organizationally, the lap-dog-size church has moved just beyond the framework of one single-cell group. Yet pastor and people are still very close.

This kind of parish is the dream fostered in most seminaries. It's the size of church that's the focus of much Sunday-school literature. With financial stability, like a solid family in the community, this kind of church family can feel warm and comfortable—perhaps too contented to reap the vast harvest that surrounds its walls.

Yard-Dog-Size Large Church

If cat-size and lap-dog-size churches were counted together, they'd represent 95 percent of all churches. The remaining 5 percent is virtually monopolized by the yard-dog-size church, with an attendance range from 200 to 1,000. Thus, comparatively speaking, the word *large* is appropriate for this assembly of congregations, which like a Great Dane, is too big to cuddle!

Structurally, all that's necessary to upgrade from lap-dog to yard-dog-size is to place a paid staff member in each of the organizations previously run by the volunteers who have become overextended, too tired to carry the administrative needs of their program organizations! With full-time staff to give energy to coaching, coordinating, and instructing, it's possible for each organization to do more than before it had paid leadership.

This size church is usually not staff led, however. Boards and committees typically dominate the agenda setting and budgeting processes. They also direct the various programs, through such devices as a worship committee or a women's ministry board or a Christian-education council.

Lay volunteers don't have time to get it all done; they need a staff member to support them. So pastors two through seven begin overseeing music, children's Christian education, youth, visitation, women's ministry, counseling, singles, business, and so on. After seven or eight, the church begins to run out of obvious areas for another staff specialist. Besides, it's run out of conventional titles!

The staff person who directs the Christian-education apparatus occupies a strategic position, because it's under his or her leadership that most equipping for lay ministry takes place.

Unfortunately, most of these directors were trained to be academic instructors rather than supervisors of group life. Similarly, religious publishing houses think of their products as curriculum for formal learning rather than as handbooks for activity directors.

This "teaching association" approach to Christian education often does not sufficiently prioritize making classes into care units. Leaders lecture, spoon-feed, and entertain "listeners" in bigger-is-better classes. They fail to give equal attention to set up opportunities to apply the truths learned in settings where the span of care is small enough to motivate and put into practice ministry behavior.

Horse-Size Superchurch

Most yard-dog-size churches must modify their organizational structure if they move beyond 800 or 1,000. They gain the speed and power of a horse by becoming a divisionalized multi-staff group of congregations. That is, a horse-size church hires its ministers as shepherds—not for particular specialty areas like counseling or visitation, but to focus on segments of the population according to life-stages, like children, teens, young adults, mature adults, and senior adults. This structure is much like a layer cake, with each level being assigned a generalist pastor who leads all programs for one age group and oversees all volunteer organizations within that age division.

The horse-size church, with its attendance of 1,000 to 3,000, is a fairly recent historical development. In the late 1940s scarcely half a dozen churches had crossed this threshold of growth. At present about 30 of the world's churches annually enter the ranks of the super-church.[2] Their total number represents well under 1 percent of churches in existence today.

Most of the first North American churches to break and continue growing through the 1,000 barrier were Baptist, and close on their heels were the Pentecostals. Most of the pioneer superchurches used bus ministry to fuel their attendance breakthroughs. (Today, the predominant breakthrough strategies involve Sunday school, seekers services, contemporary music, and miracle services. These latter are especially popular with charismatics and Pentecostals.)

Most of the early horse-size churches followed the lead of Pastor W. A. Criswell, of First Baptist Church, Dallas, Texas. He began with the traditional Southern Baptist Sunday-school system that provides age-graded classes for both children and adults. Dr. Criswell's innovation was to apply the layer-caking concept to his staff, which until then had utilized the yard-dog structure. The result was to assign pastoral leadership for each five- or ten-year age span. These ministers were given full responsibility for the programming of all hours of every week, throughout the entire year, for their age-group division.

True, this plan sometimes disrupted family life, when divisional schedules didn't coordinate. Children went one way, teens were wrested in another direction, any twenty-year-olds still at home attended yet another program, and parents had their own classes! Nevertheless, this system provided focused and meaningful work assignments for the professional church staff, and it kept events happening—or hopping!—for the membership.

Interestingly, W. A. Criswell's First Baptist success was so widely copied by independent Baptists and publicized by church-growth writer Elmer Towns that the Southern Baptist institutions and publishing houses finally began to emulate him. Their literature now acknowledges that churches larger than 1,000 need to employ staff with divisional responsibilities.

In fact, the whole issue of organizational development for the multi-staffed church, common in the corporate world, is new to the church. It wasn't until after World War II that any churches were sizable enough to need to study divisionalization. Consequently the dynamics of this important subject area remain a great mystery to most pastors and even many seminary professors.

Elephant-Size Megachurch

At one tenth of 1 percent, only their high visibility makes the next size up of interest. When a church is situated to grow larger than a horse-size church, the role of staff members often shifts to perpetual fire fighting, as doing ministry to laypeople overwhelms them.

When a church reaches between 3,000 and 6,000 in attendance, it has gained enough weight to be as ponderous as an elephant. Even with many layer-cake levels to divide the work, the organization cannot carry the load at each level without additional help. Support staff and functional specialists are hired within each growing division, even as in the yard-dog-size church, for music ministry, counseling, drama, and so on.

Although some elephant-size churches have, at this point, divided the constituency geographically, through multiple campuses, the majority maintain the organizing pattern of subdividing their constituency into medium-size gatherings. They often become a menagerie of cat- and dog-size subcongregations, each more or less self-perpetuating, resembling small churches within a church.

The adding of staff is not as simple as giving each age-level a new set of helpers all to itself! In a manner that resembles the pseudo-matrix plan found in the business community, each of these additional staff members may start with assignments as trainers–resourcers across several divisions. One person, for example, may support each age level's recreation program. Someone else may serve as coordinator for an

Evangelism Explosion training ministry to be implemented in several divisions.

Such a church dwarfs the superchurch, much as the muscle and hulk of an elephant overshadow a horse. Consequently, Christian strategists have pegged these assemblies with a new name taken from *mega-,* a prefix that means "huge." If a sports star makes a megabuck salary, and an arsenal of TNT explosives comprises a megaton, then a gigantic church is appropriately called a *megachurch.*

Obviously, it's no easy task to structure a church so the staff doesn't step on one another's toes, argue about unfair sharing of rooms or finances, or misinterpret one another's program goals! Even though each divisional group of ministers and staff serves the whole church by focusing on its own little organizations, these workers can too quickly become burned out, competitive with one another's programs, and frustrated as people fall through the cracks.

These structural limitations are a symptom of why only a dozen or so churches on this continent have topped the 6,000 level. At the time of this writing, only two of those churches have significantly passed 10,000 in average weekly attendance: First Baptist Church, Hammond, Indiana, southeast of Chicago, and Willow Creek Community Church, South Barington, Illinois, northwest of Chicago. Neither one exceeds the 20,000 mark.

As I've consulted with or near a number of this continent's megachurches, I've observed a troublesome phenomenon. Pastors, staff, and laypeople are so tired that they can't imagine how anyone would want to experience further numerical growth.

In short, the North American megachurch as we have known it seems to have come up against a ceiling; many in its leadership want to pull back, unable to keep pace with the vision of reaching an ever-growing unchurched population. Is there any light ahead? How can leaders keep the megachurch peak from becoming a dead end?

Metropolis-of-Mice Meta-Church

Although the North American megachurch seems to have stalled, the next size up is already in existence. Examples of it, each with attendances of 30,000 or more, are located in Seoul, Korea (nine of them!); Santa Fe (80,000); Buenos Aires, Argentina (70,000); Lagos,

Nigeria (70,000); Santiago, Chile (50,000); Manila, Philippines (35,000); and Rio de Janeiro, Brazil (30,000).[3]

The roots of this kind of growth are neither new nor limited to these particular cultures. The beyond-huge church tried to get started in Jerusalem, as recorded in Acts 2. In Great Britain, John Wesley launched the class-meeting movement, which embodied this explosive-growth sort of principle.[4] In China, a house-church system mush-roomed when the Cultural Revolution shut down most churches. And in North America, a number of churches (three of which are described in Chapter 12) are restructuring so as to begin the journey toward growth greater than a megachurch.

If the mature 30,000-plus type of church were likened to an animal, we'd have to create a new one! Not even the largest creatures ever to inhabit the earth, the 80-foot brontosaurus or the 100-foot blue whale, will do! Although the 14-foot elephant is small by comparison to either of these, the analogy breaks down, because gigantic animals are too fragile and liable for extinction! One infected dinosaur tooth, and the beast can die. One harpoon blast, and the whale becomes dinner meat.

What kind of mammal is durable and adaptable and can reproduce almost interminably? The answer is found in vast colonies of little creatures like rabbits or mice. I envision the beyond-huge church, therefore, as a metropolis-wide convention of mice-size groups. The term *mouse* contains added significance in that each of these furry balls of life, as introduced at the beginning of this chapter, represents a tiny, home-based cluster of believers.

What's a technical name for this next form of church? Missionary anthropologist Paul Hiebert, a colleague for several years at Fuller Theological Seminary School of World Mission, suggested the term *meta-* for the next logical category, as in progression: microtheory, macrotheory, and then *meta*theory, where sizes were supplemented by theories about theories. The prefix *meta-* means "change," as in *me-tabolism, meta*morphosis, *meta*physical, and the Greek word *metanoia* ("to change one's mind" or "repent").

The name *Meta-Church*, then, is quite distinct from megachurch. This new label allows for greater numbers, but its deepest focus is on change: pastors' changing their minds about how ministry is to be done, and churches' changing their organizational form in order to be free from size constraints. A Meta-Church pastor understands how a church can be structured so that its most fundamental spiritual and emotional support centers never become obsolete, no matter how large it becomes overall.

A Meta-Church could be, as it grows, the size of a large church, superchurch or megachurch. But because its potential scale of operation so far exceeds these other classes of churches, it should have its own name, whatever its size. (*See* Chart 2.)

The most well-known assembly of believers that illustrates Meta-Church principles is Yoido Central Full Gospel Church, in Seoul, Korea. In 1990, it encompassed some 625,000 parishioners who gathered during seven Sunday-worship services any given week. A total of 650,000 people regularly participated in home groups for Bible study and prayer.

Years ago, its pastor, Paul Yonggi Cho, became dangerously ill and had to be hospitalized for an extended time. He had developed, by exertion and faith, a several-thousand-member assembly and was suffering from physical and nervous breakdown as a result.

During his convalescence, as his parishioners visited him and sought direction, he would say, "I'm too sick to carry on the work. You must call the people together in groups and see that their needs are cared for." Many of Dr. Cho's lay leaders, especially women, felt they could not do this. He responded, "You must, under orders and permission from me." He gave them a distinctive uniform to wear. "You are not violating the Scriptures about usurping authority rebelliously [1 Timothy 2:9–15]," he explained, "because this clothing represents that you are acting as your pastor's representative."

This strategy, resorted to by a man in desperate straits, was unconventional for a Korean church. When Pastor Cho grew well enough to return to his flock, he found it thriving! Had he followed conventional wisdom, he would have apologized to the people for asking them to be in these home groups during his absence. But through prayer and wise advice, he used this almost accidentally discovered system of home groups and corresponding leadership training to lead Yoido Full Gospel to become the largest church in the history of Christendom, topping 100,000 in 1979 and continuing to enlarge.

What causes the Meta-Church principle to be so attractive? Why do people bypass churches of every lesser size to participate in a metropoliswide, convention-of-mice church? How does a developing

Meta-Church function in its embryonic stages and as it progresses toward numerical maturity? What needs to happen for the typical church of fifty to make a transition into the Meta-Church model?

I have no desire to create a clone of Pastor Cho's church or any other Oriental or Third World model here in Western society. But I've realized that something incredibly healthy is happening in these churches that often eludes even dynamically growing smaller "mission" churches. My discovery, in short, is that the organizational principle of a Meta-Church allows a church to maintain quality, no matter how much numerical success it experiences. Unfortunately, this Meta-Church model fundamentally conflicts with how most North American Christian leaders have been taught to think!

If Earth's future is to include a visible advance of Christianity, I believe the dynamics behind the Meta-Church phenomenon will need to be replicated in many densely populated world-class cities. The rest of this book, therefore, will discuss, analyze and offer practical examples of what the Meta-Church is all about.

NAME	META-ZOO	SIZE	STRUCTURE
House Group	Mouse	3-35	V V=Volunteer Leader G=Generalist Pastor
Small Church	Cat	35-75	G S=Specialist Pastor or Program Staff
Medium Church	Lap Dog	75-200	G V V V
Large Church	Yard Dog	200-1,000	G V S V S V S
Very Large Super Church	Horse	1,000-3,000	G G G S S G G
Huge Mega-Church	Elephant	3,000-10,000	S S S G G S S S G G G
Beyond Huge	Dinosaur?	10,000+	PVC CEO — Board / Worship Producer GTF / Infra-structure VHS / Administration / Office
Meta-Church?	Convention of Mice!		

Chart 2 **Find Your Church in the Zoo!**

SECTION II

The Meta-Church Model

4
Compare Tradition to Meta-Church

The term *Meta-Church,* presented at the conclusion of the previous chapter, signifies both a *change of mind* about how ministry is to be done and a *change of form* in the infrastructure of the church.

Meta- and "huge" don't necessarily go together. Meta-Church principles lead to a recognizable organizational framework, a social architecture without inherent expansion limits. If implemented properly, very large growth can result. But any size church can begin the transformation into a Meta-Church.

Because the Meta-Church idea involves a fresh mode of thinking, we'll first review some patterns found in traditional models of ministry. Which of the following are true of your church? Which do you think should be changed?

True? *Problem?*

☐   ☐   1. The most important weekly event is a worship service in which a professional minister "provides" and the laypeople "take."

☐   ☐   2. Outsiders too often view church as socially irrelevant to their personal needs.

☐   ☐   3. Newcomers (other than relatives of existing members) experience a struggle with being accepted—feeling "in."

☐   ☐   4. Those who quit the church tend to complain about a lack of caring by members and leaders.

☐   ☐   5. The church's lay leaders seem to have lost touch with the heartbeat of the founder(s) of the denomination or movement.

☐   ☐   6. The church gravitates toward a bureaucratic style that's resistant to innovation.

☐   ☐   7. The pastoral leadership controls church operations so carefully that lay efforts to develop ministry are easily discouraged.

☐   ☐   8. Attendance studies suggest that a large portion of the membership loses its church loyalty over an extended period of time.

☐   ☐   9. A commonly held expectation is that one professional pastor is required to effectively care for each 75–150 regular attenders.

The Meta-Church model will provide a new set of lenses for viewing, explaining, and handling the issues raised in this quiz. The first step, the focus of this chapter, is to present the big picture: how Meta-Church philosophy differs from traditional paradigms of ministry.

In the process, you'll learn why it is difficult to incorporate portions of Meta-Church methodology into an existing church in the same eclectic manner you assimilate other church programs. Such adaption meets with consistent frustration and produces only marginal results.

Understanding the Meta-Church is like the awakening experienced by the famous Catholic missionary Francis Xavier. Overwhelmed by the teeming masses in Asia's multitudinous cities, he wrote this message to those ministering back home under the limitations created by Roman Church structure: "Give up your small ambitions!" He had seen a reachable harvest that exceeded anyone's previous imagination.

Such is the call to those who've gazed through the refocused lenses of the Meta-Church paradigm. Such is the report from huge churches now appearing in certain of the world's population centers, growing at rates that astonish all observers, which show the use of Meta-Church principles. Such is the effective and expanding church of the future.

Meta-Church Model

The two most visible elements of a Meta-Church are the small, home-based group (to be discussed in detail in Chapters 6–9) and the celebration-size group.

Cell Level

The first group is an ongoing relational gathering—a little flock or cell—in which about ten participants model and learn how to care for one another. They receive the Lord Jesus Christ as Savior. They study the written Word of God and apply its teaching to their lives. They experience the ministry of the Holy Spirit as they build up and encourage one another. Healthy small groups combine evangelism, spiritual nurture, and calling to service.

Cells can be comprised of couples, single adults, men only, women only, or any combination thereof. Whatever the grouping, members will learn the things that will make their family life or single life work better. They'll discuss other kinds of concerns that they feel deeply about.

The leader of each home-cell group receives careful training and supervision. In fact, the net effect of all these lay ministers combined is what drives, perpetuates, and ensures the quality of the entire church!

The role of the church staff is to effectively manage the leadership development structures. *By organizing the caring and the leadership formation around the building block of a ten-person cell, a church of any overall size can insure quality or care at very intense levels.*

In years past, when Sunday schools formed a growth foundation for many churches, the usual pattern was that the senior pastor led the teachers and workers by spending significant time in planning meetings with them. This principle hasn't changed for home groups. They will succeed only if the senior pastor stands in the middle of the movement to empower it, give it vision, and make it a key thrust as important as the worship service (and supportive of it).

At the same time, the metagrowth system of organization shifts focus away from an all-too-common overdependence on overfunctioning clergy. I'm not criticizing pastoral staff who work so hard and with such dedication that they're exhausted almost to the point of burnout. I'm asking if this situation has to exist and if it's necessarily what God wants! Could it be that some of the pervasive weaknesses of North American churches stem from the inadequate organizational structures we've traditionally used?

The focus in the Meta-Church is the people: How are the disciples thriving? How well are they being cared for and encouraged by one another? The answers to those questions entirely depend on what happens in the cells and in the cell-leader training.

The activity of cells will reveal an enormous amount of flexibility and innovation, but the bottom-line result will be similar: The most significant church ministry manifests itself as changed lives in the context of a small community of believers who use their gifts to serve their group and their world.

Only on the cell level can people's deeply felt care needs be met. At any larger-size level, needs cannot be covered adequately, and the professional leader is destined for failure and criticism.

Celebration Level

The second visible dimension in a Meta-Church is the corporate celebration. Cell groups will seem to lack significance if they're not joined to (or alternated with) a praise celebration of worship.

Because of the solid relationships built in the home-cell groups, the worship celebration demands no size limitations. In fact, the bigger the better! It's like a professional football game. The stadium may be packed with 70,000 people, but how did each person get there? Probably through one or two carloads of friends who have a tailgate party and then sit together to "participate" in the cheering.

Many vital experiences take place in the cell groups, but certain other adventures in faith do not occur easily among ten people. When believers come together in a huge crowd, for example, an extra festival-like dimension of excitement attaches itself to the singing of praise or the preaching of Scripture. Also a sense of significance emerges in the consciousness of the group, an apprehension that God is accomplishing something big enough to be worthy of their involvement and investment. Finally, celebrations provide an opportunity for special events (drama, guest speaker or musician, and so on) not available to a small group assembled in a home.

This cell-celebration model resembles in some ways the pattern of worship for the nation of Israel. As they occupied the Promised Land, God's people settled by tribes in little towns. They worshiped with their extended families in their homes and, beginning with the exile, in local synagogues (the word means "congregation"). According to tradition, a synagogue could be started with as few as ten Jewish men.

The Israelites also gathered in huge numbers, at regular intervals during the year, for the festivals, feasts, and sacrifices associated with their holy days (Exodus 23:14–17; Deuteronomy 16:16, 17). The Psalmist depicts what a high point these great assemblies were: "I will fulfill my vows to the Lord in the presence of all his people, in the courts of the house of the Lord—in your midst, O Jerusalem. Praise the Lord" (Psalm 116:18, 19).

The Traditional Church Model

In contrast to this cell-celebration paradigm of a Meta-Church, the typical existing church follows some form of a (Sub) Congregational–Clerical pattern (*see* Chart 3).

A (Sub) congregation is a group bigger than a cell but smaller than a celebration. It often tries, without the greatest success, to bridge both worlds: to be intimate and caring and like a cell and to generate the excitement and festival effect of a celebration.

The ease with which congregation-size groups operate helps explain why the vast majority of North American churches level off at an

As seen in larger churches

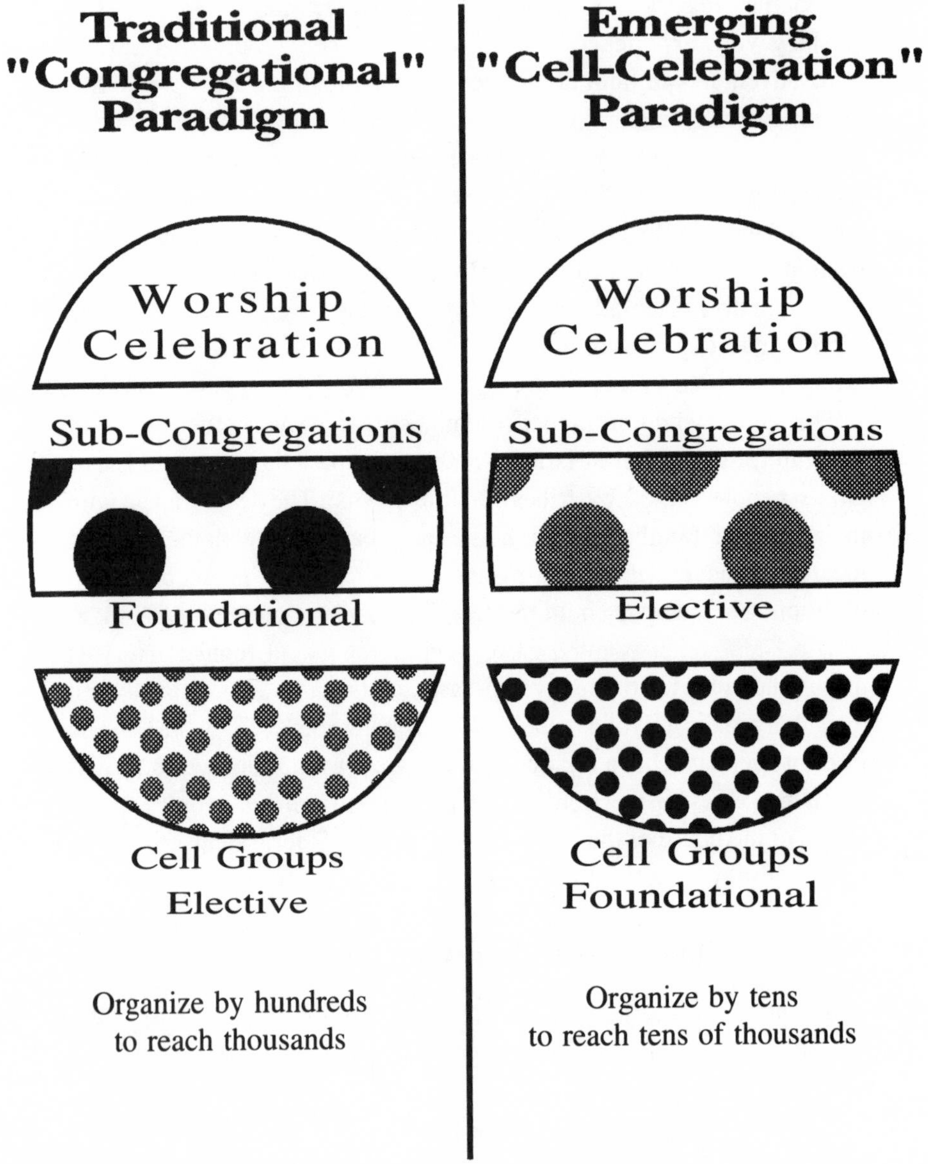

Traditional "Congregational" Paradigm

Emerging "Cell-Celebration" Paradigm

Worship Celebration

Worship Celebration

Sub-Congregations

Sub-Congregations

Foundational

Elective

Cell Groups
Elective

Cell Groups
Foundational

Organize by hundreds
to reach thousands

Organize by tens
to reach tens of thousands

Chart 3

(Sub) Congregation Levels

Wagner's Typology of Group Sizes

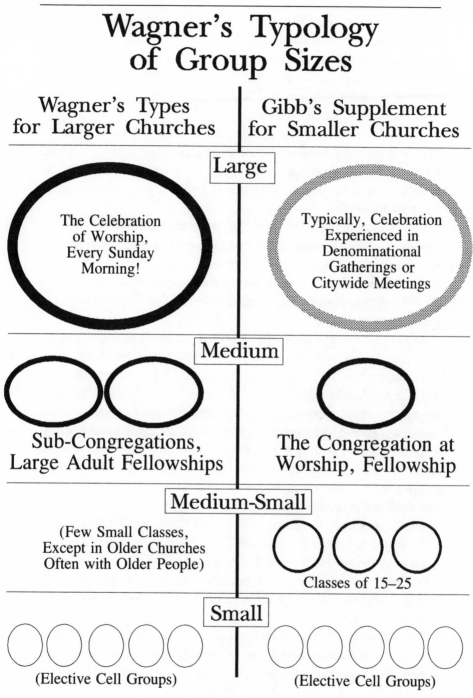

Wagner's Types for Larger Churches	Gibb's Supplement for Smaller Churches

Large

The Celebration of Worship, Every Sunday Morning!

Typically, Celebration Experienced in Denominational Gatherings or Citywide Meetings

Medium

Sub-Congregations, Large Adult Fellowships

The Congregation at Worship, Fellowship

Medium-Small

(Few Small Classes, Except in Older Churches Often with Older People)

Classes of 15–25

Small

(Elective Cell Groups)

(Elective Cell Groups)

attendance of between 50 and 100. Similarly, many sizable churches that can't seem to become even larger often behave, in actuality, like a cluster of 50–100 person congregations (what Chapter 3 called lap-dog-size and cat-size churches). Various congregation-size classes meet at a single location for Sunday school and then share in a combined-congregation worship service.

Most of these (Sub) congregations don't realize that the very fact of their size makes a number of their goals difficult to achieve. Despite Christian leaders' best intentions, the structure of their churches can contribute to feelings of indifference and attitudes of "No one really cares about me."

Such local churches may enjoy big celebrations like citywide rallies or denominational conventions. But they perceive the congregation-size gatherings as the more important, lest people feel uncomfortably lost in a crowd. Further, church leaders wrongly assume that the same festival effect is possible in a congregation of 50–100 as in a crowd of hundreds or thousands.

Ministers who lead congregations often genuinely struggle with the view that a small-group system is the best care forum. Feelings of competition, hostility, and disdain occasionally erupt between the leaders of a hundred (congregation) and leaders of ten (cell). Pastors are sometimes afraid to commission lay ministers to supervise cells for fear that they will lose the strokes that come from being the only chief.

Instead, clergy tend to view cells as helpful for those who seem to need them. If someone doesn't have a family, if he or she is too new in town to have friends yet, if an individual has counseling needs but can't afford a psychiatrist, then cells are nice to participate in. Are they essential? No, only the congregation level is, say most clergy.

From the congregation's perspective, an ever-present tendency is what I call the sand-dollar effect. The most recognizable feature of the sand dollar is a starlike design embossed in the center of its back, which seems to have been created by stitching the outline of five points.

Like the sand dollar's star embossing, a series of overlapping cliques of people are found within a church durably bound together by past experiences, common interests, and family ties. The rest of the church occupies the spaces outside of this close, clannish structure of friendships and alliances. These peripheral, marginal people are participants

Sand-Dollar Syndrome in Sub-Congregations

Long-time members are closely gathered in cliques. The interlocking of these cliques forms the informal power structure of the Congregation.

Newcomers who do not gain entry into a related clique within a short time will feel marginal, and be susceptible to dropout.

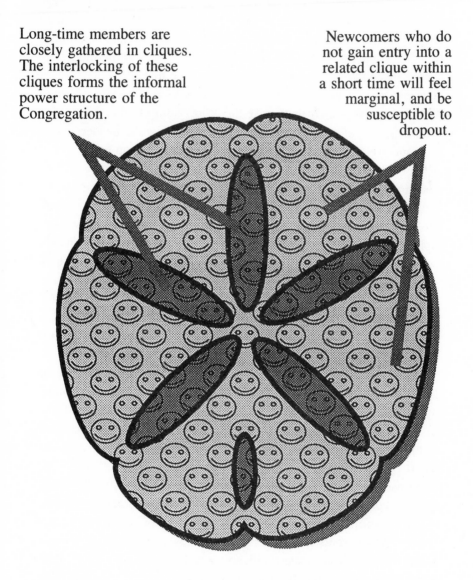

Chart 4

Sand-Dollar Syndrome

in the subcongregation, or sand dollar, but they know they're not insiders. (*See* Chart 4.)

The star insiders or cliques constitute the fueling body of the subcongregation and make it behave, in effect, as a church within the church. The people who comprise it, usually long-term or founding-father types, have been interlocked for some time. These people may or may not be the current officers or teachers, but their nod determines whether anything is actually going to happen. They know the difference between kings, because they are the king makers.

Newcomers who attempt to assert themselves find that they have to fight for acceptance. If they make the proper alliances and friendships with members of one of the cliques who constitute the insider group, they survive. If they don't, they feel alienated and drop away.

New members can't forcibly break into a clique; it must willingly open to them. If they weren't part of the clique's formation, or if the political chemistry isn't just right, or if someone else has just entered the only available clique opening, then they find themselves in a peripheral zone. The long-termers have concluded that people in that peripheral zone aren't very durable and can't be trusted. After all, they seem to hang around for a while, make a few critical comments, and then drop out or quit in disgust!

Without realizing it, these cliques form the core of a church within a church; they comfortably minister to one another but have institutionalized neglect for the marginal people.

In the process this system also gives rise to a bureaucratic style of lay leadership, because authority is derived from position and seniority. When clans and cliques carry all the clout, a church can do business as usual, whether or not its people are learning to minister or are fulfilling the original evangelistic goals of their denomination or movement!

Instead, the prime value for such churches is to conserve the "right ways," handed down from the preceding generation of power brokers.

Let me affirm that I don't oppose the existence of congregation-size groups. As a care tool, however, such groups are inadequate, even if a congregation installs class officers, who are to "make sure" care takes place. No doubt, the installation of a social and fellowship director for an adult Bible class is one possible "fix" for attempting to reach out to marginal attenders; unfortunately, this doesn't work, because one person (or two) attempts to do the job for the whole. In other words, such a person is still operating within the 50–100 size group as the primary organizational unit, so the inherent problems of limited intimacy and limited accountability in such group-size meetings are nevertheless present.

What, then, are the cat-size and lap-dog-size groups good for? Many purposes: social mixers for making acquaintances, attraction points for outsiders, forums for teaching certain academic information, or opportunities to recruit and direct people into cell ministry.

If a church has a strong need to continue its congregation-size meetings, then keep them! But repurpose the group so it doesn't become a dead-end road or an organism with a life of self-satisfaction. Make sure the group is serving some greater purpose, such as feeding people into smaller groups that can enable deeper care.

The Clergy Element

The clerical part of this paradigm deals with the issue of people's dependence on a pastor. What attitudes are revealed when certain members go elsewhere for church on the weeks that their minister is away? What percentage of the parishioners prefer to talk only with the pastor about their problems? If someone is hospitalized and ten lay-people pay a visit, does an ordained church staff member still need to drop by, in order for the sick person to feel that the church cares? Generations of clergy have worked diligently to preserve this expectation.

The underlying assumption behind these attitudes is that a pastor or skilled lay leader can provide adequate care for a group of 50–100. In reality, he or she cannot. What actually transpires is a limited intimacy and a limited accountability. Over time, many people grow dissatisfied and disillusioned, not understanding why it's so hard to go deeper in feelings of caring and belonging.

Another harmful side effect involves gift suppression. Generally anyone, clergy or lay, who can maintain the attention of up to one hundred people possesses unusual abilities. Even if this individual utilizes an array of preaching or teaching tools to involve the other ninety-nine people, this basic concept remains: "My full pitcher is pouring into your empty pitcher." In terms of spiritual gifts, one person "gives," and the primary assignment of the other people, gifted though they may be, is to take.

That's how the system has been set up. The congregation-size unit makes for structured neglect of the kind of deep hurts many people carry. It does so by preventing meaningful, widespread gift usage and by assuming that most people aren't very needy!

What would happen, for instance, if Maria, a member of a 100-person Sunday-school class for the last two years, walks into the classroom and says, "Joe packed up and left me this week"? She blurts it out and quickly is surrounded by seven or eight incredulous empathizers or gawkers, who say, "Oh, dear, really?" So during this coffee time before class, when everyone normally chats about the weather or the sports teams, Maria bawls her heart out.

Whether the circumstance is a spouse's leaving, a relative's dying, an employment termination, a pregnant teenage daughter, or any other kind of personal emergency, the large-class members and teacher each think, *I ought to help you. We need to sit down and talk. Somebody should give you a hug. I want to listen and share what God taught me during a similar crisis.*

But there are 99 others waiting to be taught—and to receive ministry! If everyone in this 100-person class went through a time of personal distress just once every two years (that is, every 104 Sundays), then Maria's outburst could be repeated weekly. If that happened, what could the teacher do? Is there an option other than to verbalize a trite, "Bless your heart; let's have a word of prayer for you" and then move on?

Given the size of the group, the more likely sequence is that many a hurting person feels embarrassed, intimidated, fearful of fueling gossip, and a bit distrustful of some of those present. As a result, reluctance overcomes the desire even to voice the heartache.

Statistics suggest that many Christians experience this battle to be accepted and cared for. One leader of a large church told me somewhat ruefully that their two-year "stick rate" for new members was 30 percent. In other words, after going through the membership procedure, seven out of ten dropped away within twenty-four months. And this church is well-known for the large number of its subcongregation-size adult Bible-study groups. Why did seven out of ten disappear? It's harder than it should be to "get in" to the caring level of most churches.

The congregation paradigm describes most of North American Christian religion, and it's failing. Why? Because it's not prepared to cope with the quality of turmoil people are experiencing in their personal lives.

What makes pastors and lay leaders dare to imagine that the existing forum of congregation-size gatherings allows for quality caring? Our traditional way of viewing what ministry is has blinded us to the needs of the people God sends our way. The circumstance of widespread dismay should compel our mind-sets to change. A shift in paradigm must occur first in the heads of church leadership. Then it must be translated into a new framework of church organization.

If this does happen, we're on the way toward becoming a Meta-Church, the kind of church desperately needed for the future.

5
Consider the Meta Advantages

Future chapters will examine the how-tos of Meta-Church ministry, but first I want to explain what can happen if church leaders understand ministry through the cell–celebration framework. Metagrowth concepts can help with a surprising number of problematic issues.

So far, I've chronicled some widespread changes in our society and predicted that the typical church cannot accomplish what God has called it to do, much less even survive, unless it deals with certain pressing issues (Chapter 1). Then I reviewed a number of church-growth strategies and suggested that the healthy, reproducible ones embody a form of the group-within-a-group idea presented later in this book (Chapter 2). Next, I outlined the organizational systems of different-size churches and concluded that some will experience a decreased quality of care as the church enlarges (Chapter 3). Finally, I introduced the Meta-Church as the model of the future: Its basic care unit, the cell, is small enough for stable, meaningful care giving yet flexible enough that its structure can assure caring cells in every church size from small to beyond huge (Chapter 4).

In this chapter I want to elaborate on four key concepts encompassed by the Meta-Church system: how believers develop a sense of belonging, how newcomers follow certain paths in their journey toward assimilation, how different-size groups contribute to different behaviors, and how numerical growth can keep from choking out pastoral care.

I'll demonstrate why each of these complex issues could be meaningfully addressed, if clusters of about ten people each become the spiritual and emotional center for a church.

This small-group proposal represents a long-term solution as well: If implemented properly, not only does the cell method build enduring organizational renewal into itself, but it is never to be repented of. The cell-care unit functions the same way, to the same benefit, across all sizes of membership. A Meta-Church can grow in scale to virtually any overall attendance level, because the locus of its most important work remains unchanged over the entire growth span of the church.

Sense of Belonging: Village or Camp?[1]

In your church, do newcomers have a hard time feeling accepted? Do people drop away because they never sense they truly belonged? Here are two analogies to help you understand the patterns believers tend to follow.

Long ago in northern Europe, thousands of small *villages* remained unchanged for centuries. Babies were baptized into the Christian heritage, within sight of the cemetery where they would one day join all their relatives. Wars and famine came and went, but church life evidenced no perceptible change from generation to generation.

At eleven o'clock each Sunday, the parish minister opened the church doors, rang the bell, administered the sacraments, and delivered a sermon that interpreted to the faithful the reasonableness of their traditions. He performed baptisms and marriages, gave catechism classes and last rites, and otherwise rarely interfered! Whether or not he was a presentational disaster, the fixed liturgies almost guaranteed that quality would remain the same. His role was clear, and it included neither establishing the village nor organizing the church.

The North American frontier pastor represented a different social convention called the *camp meeting*. Worshipers met in a makeshift tent erected for a transitory gathering of people who didn't necessarily know one another. Few valued order, tradition, or maintaining orthodoxy nearly as much as an experience of spiritual power and a sense of the immediacy of God.

The minister, usually called a "preacher," exhorted his listeners to holiness and needed charisma more than predictability. He had to gather the people, and they depended on being stimulated by his oratory, by the working of emotions or miracles, and by manifestations of the Holy Spirit. The unforeseen tended to prevail, and both minister and people placed much stock in heartfelt religion with tangible spiritual experience.

In the old villages, a sense of belonging is assumed, even from before birth, prearranged by churchgoing parents. Children increase in knowledge until their first communion, when their experience with Christ is ritualized into a sacramental form. Villagers, young and old, affirm, "I can never remember a time when I wasn't a Christian."

By contrast, camp people don't automatically belong. Their religious gatherings are ever forming and ever changing. They hear stories and witness events that influence them to conclude, "Wow! Look at all God is doing in this assembly." One day these encounters become personalized: "You know, that made a believer out of me. From that experience on, I knew Christ is real."

The camp-meeting follower now needs an understanding, just like the blind man whom Jesus healed and then later asked, "Do you believe in the Son of Man?" The man replied, in effect, "You're the one who changed my life. You tell me who this person is and I'll believe, since it comes from you." (*See* John 9:1–38.)

In camp meetings, people feel they've met God, but they're uncritical and undiscerning about how they articulate the spiritual moving they feel. They tend to accept any plausible teaching from their minister, who's earned credibility by mediating their darkness-to-light conversion.

To belong and be accepted, people in camp meeting must give a testimonial and tell the story of their religious experience, using the words they've been given for interpreting the experience and affirming the accompanying beliefs. In response, the community extends tokens of acceptance (applause, friendship, membership, baptism, and so on), resulting in a sense of belonging for the newcomers.

In today's mobile society, church leaders are discovering that more people will follow the camp-meeting pattern and require a camp-meeting type of leadership than fit into the village-church circumstance of being born into the right family.

A visitor, therefore, needs to be helped to tell his or her story to a group of members who will empathize, identify themselves as fellow travelers, and make the person feel accepted. If these circumstances occur, outsiders become insiders, even though they may express hesitations or small differences in belief; the key is for them to indicate that they're searching for and open to embracing the same things the others are.

The cell groups of the Meta-Church are like the story-telling times at camp meetings. Someone can share a spiritual experience, and the hearers can respond, "Welcome. You're one of us; we're glad you came." Instead of having to fight for acceptance, incoming guests quickly develop that all-important sense of belonging, thanks to the dynamics of small-group ministry.

Entrance to the Fellowship: Side or Front Door?[2]

When newcomers become involved in your church, what type of entry point do they most frequently pass through?

If a newcomer's initial experiences of a church are in the main worship services or to the church's on-premises programs of adult Sunday school, seasonal pageants, seminars on types of intent, community food pantry ministry, and so on, we have come to call it a "front door" entry.

A front-door admission occurs when the guests come in response to advertising or word-of-mouth invitation or helping outreach that has touched them. But it's considered front-door entrance unless, prior to coming, some level of participation and acceptance within a small group is involved.

Of this front-door crowd, what needs to happen if they're to move from passive spectators to connected members to active recruiters? Most pastors strategize ways to assimilate these newcomers by moving them from the large-group setting to smaller, more personal gatherings. A pastor's class is often the next logical step to encourage involvement. From there the entrants might be directed into various middle-size fellowship groups. From these they might be invited into the smaller cell groups, where closer relationships can develop. From that base, given time and training, they accept challenges to service, even participate in evangelism teams that issue front door invitations!

What are side-door entrants? Their relationship to the group life or community of the church is developed in the context of a friendship with a lay pastor or cell-group member, away from the church, whether from natural web-of-influence contacts or from intentionally targeted prospect pools. They generally receive a "cook's tour" of the church as their cell, which has become a binding social context, comes to church activities at the church campus. With such an introduction, they'll feel comfortable enough to return regularly.

Usually, the secret of a successful side-door entry isn't that the visitor falls in love with the worship service, but that the member accompanies his or her friends into a group that's part of the church infrastructure. From there the side-door entrant advances into deeper and deeper levels of caring involvement with the people of the cell and comes to identify with the church, participating in its subcongregation and worship services. (*See* Chart 5.)

Whichever entrance is used, notice the common element that helps new people assimilate and identify with the church: groups, particularly the ten-or-so-person cell group. For maximum effectiveness in newcomer assimilation, a church needs quality, caring groups.

Most American churches have wide front doors and attempt to catch people before they fall through the cracks. As our churches pass the 10,000 mark, they will see greater numbers coming through the side doors of cells.

Comfort Zones: Big, Mid, Small, or All?[3]

Your church, whatever its size, contains a host of different personalities: extroverts and introverts, organizers and nurturers, involvement seekers and bench warmers. These people range from first-time visitors to lifelong members. What can your church leadership do so that the largest possible percent of these people successfully lodge in, stay with, and take part in parish life?

I believe, with Peter Wagner, that churches that offer people a variety of group-size choices will better retain growth than fellowships that offer fewer options. More important, I'm convinced that the kind of group that does the best job of "keeping" people is the mouse-size home-cell group.

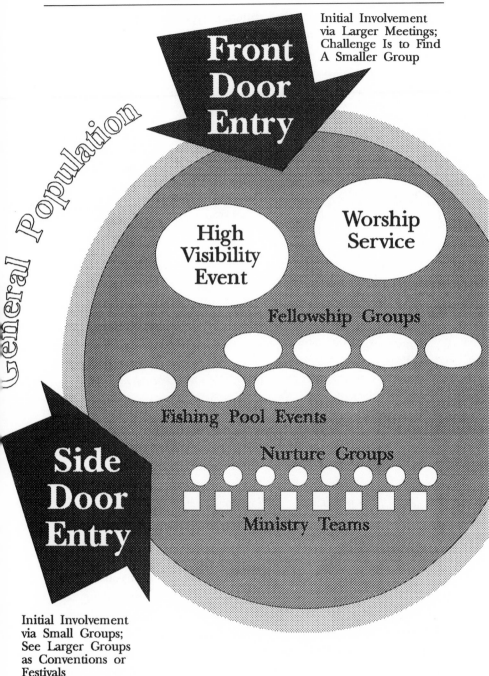

Initial Involvement
via Larger Meetings;
Challenge Is to Find
A Smaller Group

General Population

Front
Door
Entry

High
Visibility
Event

Worship
Service

Fellowship Groups

Fishing Pool Events

Side
Door
Entry

Nurture Groups

Ministry Teams

Initial Involvement
via Small Groups;
See Larger Groups
as Conventions or
Festivals

Chart 5

Chapter 4 introduced three different types of church gatherings: celebration, (sub)congregation, and cell. The chart below compares them one to another, highlighting the advantages of each. Depending on what people are looking for in a church, what their needs are, and what their comfort zone is, group size can sometimes help and sometimes hinder.

	Quick Definition	**Example**	**Advantages, Needs Met**
Celebration	Large all-church gathering, size should start in the 100's.*	Plenary worship service.	Corporate worship characterized by festivallike atmosphere of praise and excitement. Attraction point for newcomers (especially those desiring anonymity).
Congregation	Church-within-a-church, resembling a freestanding church body, 50–100* people.	Adult Bible fellowship with coffee pot and first-name "missed you last week" emphasis and birthday greetings.	General fellowship and family-like feeling. Acquaintance making and mixing. Gift usage for a few (the leader and officers). Potential feeder networking into the cell groups. Attraction point for newcomers, if advertised subjects or activities are of interest.

| Cell | Care group bigger than a household, about ten people. | Ongoing home Bible study and prayer group. | Intimacy. Accountability. Support. Pastoral care one to another. Gift discovery and usage. Surrogate extended family. Friendship base. Attraction point for newcomers. Hands-on prayer. Service to people and society. |

*Certain contexts may warrant an exception.

As I explained in Chapter 4, the congregation-size unit isn't essential to the Meta-Church model. It's helpful to have, however, as long as it contributes toward some larger purpose, such as feeding people into cell groups or attracting people to the church.

The biggest danger of this particular group is that it desensitizes church leaders, so they may tolerate benign neglect of marginal, peripheral people. This group may even communicate that it represents the best a church can do at meeting the inmost needs of its people.

Growth Without Choking

Pastors tend to show deep concern, and rightly so, that their flock be well-fed. If numerical growth takes place, great. If there's opportunity to create an attendance-charting system, fine. If some gifted person can fine-tune the congregation's organizational structure, wonderful. But the majority of ministers are people oriented, and their hearts and ears perk up most about emotional and relational issues: How are the sheep doing? How could I provide better pastoral care for their spiritual needs?

Few shepherds are satisfied that their entire membership is receiving adequate pastoral care at present—or that sufficient attention could be provided if the church grew further. Consequently they demonstrate a wariness that numerical success might choke *their* feeding of the flock. They wrongly assume that numerical increase must limit or thwart pastoral *care*.

The Meta-Church addresses this legitimate concern by creating an alternative social architecture. It's different from what ministers grew up with or were taught in seminary. It calls for a new set of organizational priorities, a church infrastructure of systematic pastoral care that's *people centered, ministry centered,* and *care centered.* The Meta-Church system is capable of nurturing any number of individual believers to the point where they're aware of their God-given gifts and are consistently using them to the benefit of others.

The contrast between the conventional model of pastoral care and the Meta-Church approach is illustrated by the difference between two kinds of growth seen in God's created order: fractal crystal and budding yeast.

A fractal is a variety of crystal that forms under special conditions. Fractals start with a nucleus: A certain particle becomes embedded in a kind of substance that allows similar molecules to bond to it. As these tiny molecular bits randomly travel through the air, they touch the "central seed," lodge, and begin growing.

These new surfaces, likewise capable of receiving bonding, expand into fingerlike projections as additional particles wander along and become linked. The crystal soon contains hundreds of long fingers, spreading in every outward direction and continuing to capture new materials.

The resultant circular shape has enormous fingers and a relatively small core (*see* Chart 6). Deep fissures offer pathways back to the nucleus, but it's unlikely that any particles will travel very far through these crevices. Instead, any drifting, unbonded particles are usually caught by one of the outermost fingers. The appendages capture new materials faster than the particles can wander down into the center.

Fractal crystals form beautiful patterns that can be colored according to their time of bonding. Each hue or shade can represent how recently the molecular bonding occurred. Thus the outer edges can be nearly white, the midway level another shade, and the inmost core nearly black.

Corals An example of a fractal form

Let a coral cell represent a small group. Consider long-tenured members to be fixed in cliques, so newcomers are remote from most of them. As their tenure increases, members are more involved in governance and less involved in receiving newcomers, hence a church's responsiveness declines.

Yeasts "J-Curve" population growth

Let a yeast cell represent an "open" growth group. Newest people to enter such a group come into contact with long-tenured members within it, thus influencing leaders' awareness of growth issues. To maintain small sizes, groups give birth, hence geometric growth of groups over time.

Chart 6

Many churches appear to be similar in formation to such crystals. They contain several identifiable groups that represent the different times at which they came to the church. They may be members of the same "mineral," but there's no interaction. The old guard sticks closely together at the center, only occasionally penetrated by any new faces. People's reluctance to stay open, based on when they "lodged," creates isolation of the older from the newer, the more powerful from the less mighty, the more experienced from the less trained.

Thus church veterans hold the power but are increasingly unable to relate to the changing needs represented by the newcomers. Their life stage makes them virtually irrelevant and inaccessible to the recently approaching people from the general seeking population.

Yeasts, by contrast, grow in an entirely different fashion. A yeast plant, when placed in a nutrient, begins a continual process of gestation. It absorbs the food, but doesn't grow indefinitely larger. Instead, the egg-shaped plant or cell begins to change from the inside as a protonucleus forms and a budding process begins. This swelling protrusion soon functions like an independent plant. It breaks away and bulges with new life until an entire colony exists, created as mothers and daughters drop apart, each a fully functional yeast plant as at the start.

The story of yeast is a parable of growth in a healthy church (see Chart 6). The yeast itself is analogous to a cell group: The yeast nucleus represents the cell leader; the newly forming nucleus denotes an apprentice leader; the nutrients stand for the people—the new energy and life—who come to church services, new member classes, and other learning opportunities.

Then, stirred by acquaintance devices, they're incorporated into the walls of the cells. The love of cell members one for another advertises the attractiveness of cell life both to other parishioners and to those not yet exposed to the church.

As long as a nucleus continues to replicate and the surrounding environment contains available people, the cell will continue to grow. Unlike the isolation caused in the development of a fractal crystal, as yeast bodies divide and spin off, new nutrients (analogous to unchurched or unreached people) have equal access to every yeast cell (representing the evangelistic home cells) until they are incorporated.

The nature of yeast is to multiply until the total population is more than anyone could ever dream. What if churches did likewise? Could cells of Christians continue to propagate without ill effect on the quality of pastoral care?

As I've stated previously, the largest church in Christendom exists today in Seoul, Korea, and has grown using cell-group principles. Its total involvement count exceeds 650,000 in a city of 12 million. A dozen other Seoul churches are growing rapidly, using similar techniques. Already 25 percent of the city professes to follow Christ.

Who's to say what the saturation point will be? Who's to limit any one of these churches from reaching 2 or even 5 million people? The apparent lesson so far is that systematic pastoral care *can* take place without a reduction in quality until the target population in the service area is evangelized and discipled to its fringes!

Imagine having cell-group leaders in your church who have extensive vision for aggressively recruiting apprentice leaders and forming new cells. These people pray and work together to the end that God would commission each of them to new cell activity. On and on the process continues, like the exponential growth of the colony of yeast cells.

Can you envision such a collaboration of the Holy Spirit and human leadership? It's foreign to our Western minds because we're used to a carnal form of Christianity.

The Bible says that the growth of the kingdom will be like leaven—such as yeast! (*See* Matthew 13:33.) Can we develop a church structure capable of allowing enormous growth until it has literally leavened the whole lump—whatever size community that represents?

SECTION III

How to Make Small Groups Work

6
Begin to Identify Your Mice

Remember Chapter 3's description of a "Metazoo"? It began with the mouse-size spiritual kinship group and progressed upward through various magnitudes of churches, using animals from cat (small) to elephant (huge).

The final stage, the Meta-Church, seemed to call for an animal like a blue whale or dinosaur. Instead, I suggested an unusual alternative: the image of a convention; a metropoliswide gathering of mice.

Why? A mouse, representing a mouse-size group, is durable, adaptable, and able to give birth to an additional mouse-size group in a short amount of time! Plus, a passel of mouse-size groups signifies the essence of the Meta-Church: It need not be of stupendous proportions, but a structural ability (social fabric of mouse units) that maintains quality caring no matter what scale (how many mice units) the entire church becomes.

I believe that genuine caring is the engine in each local church that propels its growth. This nurture dimension is essential to church health. If people see and experience a care-giving environment, their lives will change, and their friendship networks will be impacted as well.

Most Christians, for example, have heard a story similar to the following and silently wished that the concern it models could have originated in their own church. After chronicling this true event, taken from a church that's built on home-cell groups, I'll analyze step-by-step how this same level of care can occur within any fellowship committed to the Meta-Church model.

How Spiritual Kinship Looks

Reverend Dale Galloway, founding pastor of New Hope Community Church, Portland, Oregon, was at home when he received a telephone call summoning him to a home in his community. A grisly and bizarre murder had taken place in a distant state, and the detained suspect was the alienated foster child of one of the families in his church. The child had been troubled for some time, and even as the rest of the family had come to Christ, the youth had left home and moved to that particular state.

"These people are going to need some moral support," Pastor Galloway told his wife as he put on his jacket. "I'd better get over there and see what I can do."

When he arrived, he feared he was too late. Local news teams were already filming the house from the street, and a crowd of reporters clustered around the front door.

As he rushed up the driveway, he saw one of the members of this family's Bible study, called a Tender Loving Care (TLC) group, standing on the porch, guarding the door and detaining the journalists. The group parted to let the pastor through.

Inside, Pastor Galloway noticed another TLC-group member talking on the kitchen telephone, lining up meals for the family and screening incoming calls. He continued to the living room, where he found a third TLC caregiver comforting the family. Pastor Galloway gave the grieving family a hug, led in a prayer, and asked what else he could do. "Nothing, Pastor," they said. "Everything is under control. It was awfully nice of you to come by."

He stayed an hour, at most, and then left, praising God for the handful of men and women in the TLC group, who had learned of their friends' distress, come to the house, and begun providing meaningful ministry! Even if Pastor Galloway had been away or unable to visit, the family wouldn't have been neglected; they were being well-cared for by the lay ministers who were "supposed" to look out for their pastoral needs—their TLC group.

What principles can be gleaned from this story? First, in the perception of the grieving family, this intimate TLC group of about ten people *was* their church. Some of its members were available and able to do everything that really mattered: provide intimate care. In actuality, New Hope Community Church at that time drew about 4,500 people to its corporate worship services. But thanks to its small-group-based organizational system, the caring element was equivalent to or better than what's often found in an effective small church.

Second, relationships were developed before the crisis. Friendships were in place, and people were prepared to give and receive care. What a contrast with churches that operate under a system where a deacon or staff member receives a message, "This family's on your list; go introduce yourself and help them through their need." The heartbroken family might not have allowed access to their intimate space, and the needed support couldn't have been given.

Third, the church's delicate, sympathetic attention touched this husband and wife so deeply that six months later they enrolled in training for TLC-group leadership. They wanted to show the same kind of care to others.

How Cell Ministry Works

The rest of this chapter focuses on the activities necessary for an effective small-group system. Chapter 7 will explain how to instill a vision of pastoral care in each group. Chapter 8 will highlight certain impediments to Meta-Church cell health. And Chapter 9 will present a scriptural paradigm and strategy for leadership development.

Make Cells the Fundamental Building Block

In order for groups to assure optimal pastoral care, cell cultivation must be the central skill and discipline of everyone involved in the church. Each decision, every organizational system, and all leadership development will be evaluated in the light of their contribution to multiplying the work of the ministry through the mouse-size structures.

Such reprioritization achieves a far-reaching purpose. It maintains high responsiveness to each new person's entry and development until the target population of a church's service area is evangelized and discipled to its fringes.

Most North American churches function so differently that their leaders cannot visualize this new way of thinking. Rather, they tend to follow a departmental approach: "Cells? Yes, good idea. Let's form some small groups." They review their church's organizations and programs, find a few uninvolved people, lasso in a few others who say yes to everything, and create another program, this one for cells.

Under this compartmentalization, both leaders and participants encounter difficulty in elevating their group to highest importance. After all, most people can handle only two and a half involvements: leadership of one ministry, solid participation in another, and occasional participation in a third.

As I indicated in the congregation-clerical model of Chapter 4, a church's pastors, staff, and most visible laypeople lose their effectiveness by trying to be the spiritual guides for too great a crowd. This condition perpetuates itself through numerous church departments ever clamoring for the same few people to serve as captains. Thus the structure of most churches isn't conducive to cell cultivation.

Identify All Your Small Groups

The organizational structure of most churches is loaded with groups, but the typical pastor doesn't recognize them as such. In my opinion, the membership accomplishes almost all its real work through cell-sized groups: church board, small adult-Sunday-school classes, usher corps, women's missionary prayer fellowship, choir, worship committee, drama ensembles, youth sponsors, senior-adult program, deaf ministry, softball team, nursery volunteers, Stephen ministers, parking-lot attendants, English as a Second Language ministry, and so on.

If so, what about people who seem to operate one-on-one, such as the small-church member who volunteers in the office or the large-church adherent who sits alone in the microphone control room? Chances are, if traced to their supervisory sources, each of them does indeed belong to some small group.

In fact, if these individual lay ministers don't feel part of a small-group team, they'll soon feel isolated. They need cell interaction but don't comprehend what they lack; the result they want to experience from their ministry represents what a cell is designed to produce! To the extent these soloists are noticed, grouped, understood, and managed by the church staff, they will feel nurtured, fulfilled, and encouraged in their labors of love.

What, then, does a cell accomplish? Each one addresses four dimensions of ministry: loving (pastoral care), learning (Bible knowledge), deciding (internal administration), and doing (duties that serve those outside the group). Every type of cell, however, embodies a different mix of majors and minors on these emphases. (*See* chart 7.) Each, however, will generally fit under one of two headings: nurture groups or task groups.

Discover the Vitality of One-Another Nurture Groups

Probably the most popular class of cell is the home Bible study. Many people relate well to this kind of group, with its focus on learning, because it provides a comfortable adaptation of the teaching focus they're used to on Sundays. Caring and sharing must also be present, however, or else participants become intellectually and interpersonally sterile. The deciding component is likewise essential: When will we meet again? At whose house? Who will bring refreshments? Finally, Bible studies, especially if they've been in existence for a while, sometimes undertake service projects and other "doing" responsibilities for the entire church or community.

The agenda checklist may read: studying the Bible, worshiping through song, sharing problems and testimonies, praying, planning for the next meeting, and helping others. (*See* chart 8.) Underlying these activities, however, the same four components remain: loving, learning, deciding, and doing.

Ratios of Key Functions by Cell Group Types

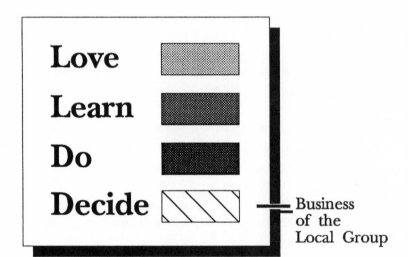

Care Group | Bible Study | Ministry Team

Growth,   Book,   Ushers,
Support   Topic,   Choir,
Groups   Other   Food Bank

Chart 7

Group Agenda: Encouragement

Using Gifts for "One Another" Ministry

-Singing
-Sharing
-Praying
-Bible
Application

Chart 8

Thus the Bible-study cell actually encompasses far more than what its name implies. That's why I classify it as a nurture or care group; its people minister one to another. Within the scope of using Scripture to teach one another, members are encouraging one another's relationships with God and people. (*See* Chapter 9's list of fifty-nine one-another commands in the New Testament.)

Support and recovery groups likewise major in nurturing. They strongly emphasize the love component, through listening and sharing. As the group matures, it may develop the "do" element as well. Anytime newcomers come aboard, however, the group backs up and adds in more of the love component. The deciding factor inevitably comes up because of the ongoing maintenance needs of the group. And the Bible knowledge factor usually occupies some portion of each meeting as well.

The most common form of support and recovery groups is the twelve-step methodology that equips people to move from sufferers to an overcomer status. Small groups provide a framework for the catharsis needed from discussing one's story and dealing with the forgiveness and relearning needed. Examples include trauma survivors (parents of homosexuals, battered wives, or incest victims), addicts (alcoholics, workaholics, or sex addicts), and many others wanting to break a cycle of dependency or codependency.

Sometimes professionally certified clinicians will head the groups or will be retained by the church to train and consult with the group leadership. Virtually every church has adherents whose problems are severe enough that they disable any healthy nurture group they join. In providing a specialized forum for helping these strugglers, a church can open the door to the droves of community people who are plagued by similar needs. Many of them are willing to participate in biblically based therapy.

Discover the Potential of For-the-Benefit-of-Others Task Groups.

Church boards, ministry teams, task forces, audit committees, and similar groups devote the majority of their efforts to making policy decisions and doing ministry for their church.

Will Bible learning be introduced in their meetings? It must if the church's discipleship responsibility is to be fulfilled. How about loving? People need mutual prayer and sharing, or they feel like automatons. Some church councils, for instance, wisely devote the opening thirty or forty-five minutes of their meeting to sharing and learning. As a result, better decisions are made by better people.

The least-trained type of for-the-benefit-of-others group tends to be the ushers; their group morale depends on their being nurtured. This kind of team building usually happens best over dessert at the leader's home. Unless the usher corps are constantly worked with and spiritually touched, their dispositions can sting with grumpiness and grouchiness!

Even my kids can accurately predict which ushers regularly blow up at people. My son and I once noticed a friendly, unfrazzled usher. "We must be here earlier than usual," my son concluded. "He'll get bad before the day is over!"

The translation into principle? If a group focuses on doing and deciding and fails to blend in loving and learning, its people's behavior will fall apart. They'll radiate everything but care.

Churches of the future must inaugurate a new type of task group that focuses on certain church people, generally the more peripheral attenders, who remain outside a group network. I believe that every forward-thinking church should regularly canvass all parishioners through the establishment of a *telecare* phone system.

The goal is to call every household once a month. The informal tests I've conducted indicate that church people appreciate a friendly call of concern; few reject it as a junk call.

A handful of churches are even experimenting with automated phone announcements: "Hi! This is the voice of Pastor Kronbach, with a one-minute tape of exciting updates on this week's church events. Then we can record prayer requests that you wish to share with our telecare teams. . . ." People are becoming more tolerant of voice mail. Even if they protect themselves by using their telephone answering machines in call-screening mode, the two machines can talk to each other, and the parishioners can respond if and when they wish to.

The preferred structure, however, is a telecare shift—a team of about five callers, who, working in a room equipped with five phone lines, make eight calls apiece over a two-hour shift. The net outcome is forty households being touched each shift as part of the church's program of total pastoral care.

The telecare system doesn't wait until a crisis develops or people verbalize their gripes about feeling neglected. It calls anyway, helping forty families to feel loved—or more loved.

What priority of phoning should telecare teams follow? First on the list are church newcomers, such as first-time guests who filled in a line on the friendship pad during the Sunday worship service. (Pew register forms that are passed down the row draw a greater participation rate than do pew cards; in addition, some churches encourage everyone to look at the pads as they're returned to the end of the row, thereby providing cell-group leaders in the row with a tool for meeting newcomers on the first day of their visit.)

Second comes the crisis needs. Sometimes the telecare team functions like a fire station: It receives a call that a fire has started. The summons could be a note or call saying, "Did you know, Pastor, that . . . ," a referral from the local hospital chaplain, or a hurting individual who responds to the church's Yellow Pages ad or mass mailings.

Other crisis-condition data can be captured by gleaning from the news media. When I pastored in a small university city with a number of hospitals, I learned that many families, disconnected from society, get into media-highlighted trouble and don't know where to turn. A sympathetic lay church contact, initiated by a phone call, may be their only offer of help.

Preferably, the telecare team will adopt the fire-inspector approach: They do checkups so as to prevent fires or detect the first smoke. The fire station "unit for the alarm bell" approach demonstrates passive care; the fire-inspector method shows active care, which is more effective.

Third priority goes to shut-ins and others who cannot get out on their own.

Fourth comes the rest of the church, both those active and those inactive.

What happens when a member of the telecare team uncovers an urgent need? "The Garcias have been laid up for a couple of months now, and they're really hurting. Somebody should go over and see them."

A computerized membership database, constantly updated and instantly accessible, should indicate whether that person is, or has been, associated with a small group. If so, the telecare team phones the group leader. If not, they dispatch the deacon ministry, which has been organized into crisis-response teams. Or they call individuals trained by the Stephen Ministry program (*see* the section on clergy and para-clergy in Chapter 8). Occasionally in older churches, if members have a high expectation that only an "official" pastor can care, the telecare team will arrange for a staff visit.

As today's financial pressure on the middle class continues, a greater percentage of church people will seek help with their basic needs of food, clothing, and rent. Increasingly, strangers will walk into the doors of the church facilities saying, "I am hungry," or "My baby doesn't have milk."

These issues will not go away soon. Rather than insulating themselves from these situations, churches must learn how to do family-services intake counseling. The Salvation Army has done this for years. Newer programs, such as Love, Inc., sponsored by World Vision, are designed to give churches a handle on coordinating their efforts with community agencies. Telecare teams can stand on the front lines of this kind of ministry.

Why can't a prayer-chain system detect and address such needs? Prayer chains work quite well in smaller churches. Everybody prays, some phone the hurting person, and a few get involved in providing support. Prayer chains work best, however, within the network of a cell system. People already know and trust each other, and they feel more free to share their personal needs.

As churches grow larger, prayer chains lose effectiveness in providing pastoral care to those not in any group. Such people need constant polling to make sure they're okay. If burglar-alarm companies can install systems to monitor whether someone's property is safe, why aren't churches using our skills to safeguard the souls of our people?

Those who join a telecare team, unless carefully monitored, can experience ministry fatigue. A church's pastoral staff, as the architects of care giving, will train the telecare leaders to involve loving, learning, deciding, and doing in their teams. If all four activities are occurring to one degree or another, the health of any type of cell group, whatever its name or function, can be assured over time.

One final, essential ingredient must be added to the dynamics of love, learn, decide, and do. This remaining factor, more than any other, will enable a church to make the quantum transformation into becoming a Meta-Church. The entire next chapter, therefore, concentrates on how to guide cells into a vision of pastoral care.

7
Structure Cells to Do Pastoral Care

The Meta-Church vision calls for far more than a church landscape that's dotted with identifiable small groups. It needs a well-developed system of quality, care-centered nurture groups, plus certain necessary task groups, maintained in optimal health for growth and reproduction.

Most Meta-Church cells will be nurture groups. Several characteristics will differentiate them from other models of small groups.

Laypeople Do the Pastoring

The leader of each nurturing group functions as a lay pastor to that ten-or-so-person flock. This shepherd takes responsibility for the spiritual vitality of the cell and receives careful oversight from the senior pastor or pastoral staff.

Cell leaders may be of either gender, even as the group may be single sex or mixed sexes. Leaders may be married or single. They may bear a church title (elder, deacon, Sunday-school superintendent, and so on), or they may not.

The one essential ingredient? Instead of being left to float along on

their own, they receive personal authorization, supervision, and training from the church staff. (Chapter 9 will amplify this process of
managing a cell group's lay leadership.)

Why shouldn't pastors themselves lead the cells? They can. All
ministers should know how to head a cell and should model that
leadership role to their parishioners. If a pastor begins to inaugurate a
Meta-Church understanding of ministry, the first step often involves
forming a group from a cadre of church pillars.

After experiencing the richness of a nurture group, some of these
people will commit themselves to beginning their own groups. Then
the pastor, instead of training ten people, will focus attention on training leaders of ten and, as soon as possible, on managing those who will
train the leaders of ten.

A pastor forges an authentic ministry by modeling contact with three
segments of society: the unsaved community, the church cell group,
and the leaders of cell groups. At every point, a minister's involvement
in a cell makes a desirable statement, but the major time and energy
investment must be in the training of leadership.

Do clergy believe that the laity, if given the opportunity, will invest
time, energy, and money to learn the skills required to do a competent
job of pastoring? I'm convinced that laypeople take ministry to a
limited-size group so seriously that they prefer a role in cell leadership
to most any other office or honorific title in a church. Laypeople want
to make a difference in a way that touches a person's inmost world!

Laypeople also provide long-range stability. If professional clergy
lead most or all a church's groups, every change of pastors destabilizes
and may derail whatever small-group system the outgoing minister had
started to build. No two Western pastors hold the same philosophy or
strategy of ministry. If an independent group of evaluators measured
the standard of consistency in North American pastoral performance,
we—and our seminaries—would be graded out of existence!

Am I implying that churches shouldn't specifically assign a staff
member to cell development? Yes and no.

As the cells fare, so goes the whole Meta-Church movement. If the
senior leadership misses the distinction between a ''cell-celebration
church'' (see Chapter 4) and a ''church with a cell ministry,'' then a
small-group specialist can do little overall good. Or if the main pastor
is simply a methodology pirate who can't perceive how the Sunday-

morning pulpit affects the Thursday-night cell group or Saturday-morning leader-training meeting, then few will catch the Meta-Church vision.

On the other hand, if *every* staff member has developed a cell consciousness and assumes a role in sponsoring and maintaining healthy cells, then it's possible for some to carry a larger responsibility for all leadership training than others without the system suffering from compartmentalization.

Pastoring Supersedes Teaching

Nurture-focused cell groups become edification centers. The Holy Spirit's gifts are operative as merciful people empathize, teachers instruct, serving people assist, prophets exhort and upbuild, and so forth. Each person will contribute something. The composite gift mix of the group will determine its particular style of encouragement.

Therefore such structures as grading systems, ten points that must be covered, and rigid agendas are taboo if they stifle the Holy Spirit's ministry. If the need for the evening cries for prayer over a group member's emotional scar or demonic oppression, then the three-point sermon must wait. The teaching gift cannot be valued above the pastoring function.

Everyone Welcomes Newcomers

Show me a nurturing group not regularly open to new life, and I will guarantee that it's dying. If cells are units of redemption, then no one can button up the lifeboats and hang out a sign, YOU CAN'T COME IN HERE. The notion of group members shutting themselves off in order to accomplish discipleship is a scourge that will destroy any church's missionary mandate.

The one exception might be groups that organize around a specific therapeutic focus. A case in point would be therapy for a sensitive developmental issue, such as child abuse. Even such groups, if they remain closed for more than a few months, however, may begin doing as much harm as good.

Groups could symbolize their evangelistic heartbeat by setting out an empty chair whenever they meet (an idea popularized by Lyman Coleman). The group will pray for the person who will next fill that chair.

As first timers feel welcomed, if they are unconverted, the love of God through this group will convict them. The Holy Spirit will influence their hearts, their resistance and reluctance will be broken down as members pray the evil one away, and these newcomers come to Christ.

When a church shifts the locus of outreach from the pastoral staff and from specialty evangelization teams to the small groups, the harvest potential becomes almost incalculable. The world's largest church, the Yoido Full Gospel Church, in Korea, enlarges its scope of ministry by about 20 percent a year. That's tens of thousands of new people, a good portion of whom are previously unchurched and unsaved, every twelve months!

The genius of Yoido Full Gospel's numerical success flows from each cell group as it grows annually by an average of just two people: from eight members to ten, or from ten to twelve, which leads to birthing new cells. That very manageable goal, when multiplied by more than 50,000 cells, produces amazing growth.

Even in a smaller church of 50, the compounding effect of cell growth alone could likewise multiply the number of people involved. A 20 percent growth rate will double the church in four years, and result in 310 people in ten years, 770 in fifteen years, and 2,358 in twenty years!

Sustained growth is possible in any church, but not because a pastor or evangelism team proclaims, "Let's reach a million people!" Rather, according to the Meta-Church model, one tenth of the membership (each lay leader in an eight-to-twelve-person cell) bears the vision and responsibility, plus the assistance of the others in the group, for bringing in two new people each year.

Lay Pastors Look Beyond Dropouts and Failures

The average church permits a low-risk, low-commitment, small-group system with short-term commitments, because it anticipates that participants will burn out and lose interest. Such a church fears saddling its people with long-term accountability. After all, what if people don't like their group, but they're too polite to say so and just drop out? Further, this church doesn't expect members to work through the conflicts of personality or style that seem inevitably to arise.

In wanting to help people avoid entrapment, the church risks their going untouched, uncorrected, unshaped, and unformed.

Meta-Church cells aren't calendared to terminate. If someone wants to get away from a fellow member with whom there's a personality conflict, and both parties can't work it out on spiritual grounds, then one of these people can be part of a daughter cell commissioned off from the group. Tensions and discontent can be motivational devices for birthing.

At the same time, cell-group veterans will understand that the nature of people work involves sinfulness, immaturity, and circumstances beyond human control. The Meta-Church system encourages every church member to be part of a group, but it reluctantly acknowledges that some participants will drop out, and some leaders, in learning more about their area of giftedness, won't continue in heading up a cell.

In my experience, no church has successfully launched a cell system without averaging three turnovers of leadership. In other words, pastors typically flounder twice with each cell-system startup before they discern and train the right person for it!

The gestation period for healthy groups to grow and divide ranges from four to twenty-four months. The more frequently a group meets, the sooner it's able to divide. If a group stays together for more than two years without becoming a parent, it stagnates. Bob Orr, of the Win Arn Church Growth, Inc., reports that groups that meet for a year without birthing a daughter cell only have a 50 percent chance of doing so. Groups meeting two years without birthing a daughter cell only have a 5 percent likelihood of doing so. But every time a cell bears a child, the clock resets. Thus a small subgroup can remain together indefinitely and remain healthy and fresh by giving birth every few months.

A small number of groups, by charter, are not expected to give birth. Examples include such for-the-benefit-of-others groups as official boards and strategic planning committees. Even they would do well to consider what a more open process could mean to orienting new leadership talent.

Everyone Pastors Better Through Off-Premises Ministry

Whenever possible, cell groups will meet somewhere other than the church facilities. There are a number of reasons to support this prac-

tice. First, as the number of cells multiplies, their off-premises locations will obviate the need for excessive building programs (more
rooms and more parking spaces). Also, settings like homes enhance
both gift usage, such as hospitality, and interpersonal development.

Most significantly, portable groups can, like a right-there-at-my-
corner McDonald's hamburger franchise, go to where the people live
and work. Christian fellowship can occur at locations and meeting
times most convenient to group members, especially as the church
draws from a larger geographical area and time and cost of travel
become significant factors. Such flexibility of scheduling will also
facilitate extra gatherings for friendship building or for extended sea-
sons of prayer.

Everyone Adopts a New Perception of Paid Pastors

Professional clergy, other paid staff, lay-class teachers, and membership must all discard the do-it-myself concept of parish ministry.
This ideal holds that a pastor can meet the personal needs of a
congregation-sized group of up to 100 people. By contrast, the vision
of the future sees each leader as working to develop lay ministers who
care for a group of ten.

Which of these views seems more strategic? At first thought, our
Western, train-the-professional-to-carry-100 ideal, appears best. But if
I want my efforts to be multiplied, not merely added, then I must live
by a concept that says, "I'll spend time with you if you're leading ten
others." It's a concept that leverages ministry. It's biblical to invest in
something that will increase one's investment! (*See* Matthew 25:14–30
and elsewhere.) It's a variant of the rule. Better to cultivate ten works
than the work of ten!

Everyone Agrees to Certain Preestablished Roles

Nurturing groups need to meet at least twice a month in order for
members to influence one another's behavior. If gatherings are less
frequent, the trust levels will remain too shallow. Participants will go
only as far as reconnecting, but won't share deeply or participate in
mutual self-examination or support.

No matter how often or for what purpose a group meets, people will begin to take on certain roles. The Meta-Church strategy intentionally structures each group to embody the following roles.

Leaders Take on Manageable Responsibilities. The leader of each ten-person cell is someone who knows how to make a group happen. This individual serves as a facilitator who convenes a cell, who knows how to deal with problem-laden people, and who possesses the skills needed to promote acceptance, friendship, and nonthreatening interpersonal vulnerability, mostly by modeling.

Leaders don't bear the label of *teacher* or any other gift-related title, because that may be the calling of someone else in the group! Their agenda typically involves worship, Bible study, sharing, and prayer, but the greatest emphasis is relating truth to life. This occurs as much through participatory discussion as through the presentation of an academic lesson. Leaders' underlying purpose is to see that participants use their gifts from the Holy Spirit to care for and encourage one another in spiritual nurture.

A second person, the understudy of the group leader, is an apprentice with the role of recruiting and motivating others toward the birthing of a new group. Does an individual with these gifts exist in a typical church? Discovery of spiritual talent is one of the most important factors in the development of a Meta-Church. The Holy Spirit promised to make gifts and gifted people available to churches for mutually edifying one-another ministry (1 Corinthians 12:4–11; Ephesians 4:3–13). The motivating Spirit of God will provide the people needed, unless He's been grieved, quenched, or otherwise prevented from working.

When the leadership apprentice is developed well enough to help form the embryo of an offspring cell, who will head it up? For long-existing groups full of established relationships, it's better to send out the apprentice whom the members have helped tutor. In recently formed groups, which are more fragile, it's often easier to send out the facilitating leader so that the apprentice can remain to strengthen and consolidate the existing group.

Never should anyone call this mitosis process a "split," since that word emphasizes a sense of loss. The birthing concept intimates opportunity. A group produces an apprentice leader and then releases that person to start a new work. If an existing member wants to go along, fine.

Otherwise, as a group takes in new blood it will eventually exceed the optimum size of ten. Quality of care will noticeably decrease above ten, because time and listening patience run out too quickly. Wise leaders perceive that the newer members will need to be launched into their own group.

Another type of leader in a small group is the occasionally visiting resource person who's serving as the coach to the leader and apprentice. This individual regularly oversees five groups and itinerates regularly from group to group, though not directing any meetings except in extraordinary circumstances.

What other leadership roles are represented in a care group? Each cell (and each being-birthed cell) will need a hospitality person to oversee arrangements for meeting site, refreshments, and social gatherings. This host or hostess handles all the elements of physical ease, while the leader concentrates on the nurture of souls. No one person can effectively carry both loads alone.

What if parents, especially single parents, want to participate in a cell but have problems financing child care? The hospitality person lines up a baby-sitter, and the entire group foots the cost or proposes some other creative solution. Laypeople are capable of solving most problems associated with ministry, although certain of their number will expect the central church staff to carry their responsibilities for them.

Should this nursery time contain spiritual education? If possible, fine, but its main purpose is to enable adults to grow in Christ so that, as one of many results, they learn to talk with their own children about the gospel.

Growing Christians Mix With Seekers. Every cell will have individuals interested in maturing as disciples of Christ. These are people who have made certain commitments to their Lord, to growth, and to the group. Also present will be men and women looking for a church, both front-door and side-door people (*see* Chapter 5), whether pre-churched seekers or Christians who don't yet feel at home in any one church.

Usually, Christians are more quickly attracted to cell groups than are seekers. The symbol of the empty chair, described earlier in this chapter, will remind those who have caught the vision for outreach to pray for newcomers and be open to them when they come.

How exciting and motivating for a group member to participate in an entire cycle from empty chair to seeker to fellow disciple to helper in ministry or even apprentice leader!

Although the apprentice carries the main responsibility for building the nucleus of a new group, all members will help with the recruiting. As they make contacts through those attracted to the middle-sized group congregations (*see* Chapter 4), and with others in their personal friendship networks, they help create fishing pools and can even tie off a few fish themselves! (I call this process a fishing-pool function. It, along with the idea of churchwide marketing, will receive attention in Chapter 10.)

Referral Systems Help With Problem Situations. About one out of every two cell groups will draw in a person who has extra needs stemming from a personal crisis, fragmented family, dysfunctional childhood, or medical neurosis. Some of these hurting members are bottomless wells who can siphon off all the love, interest, and energy an entire group can offer. If a church offers no technique or system for dealing with these people, whom Dale Galloway has called extra-grace-required (EGR) people, they will kill the group. Some won't be satisfied, and they require more care than the leader can provide.

How to deal with them? As soon as a chronic EGR begins draining the energy out of a leader, the leader's coach will become involved. Perhaps the leader and coach together will sense that the EGR cannot heal in a normal group, and they'll recommend referral to a recovery or support group. In severe cases they may need to take part in a clinician-led group or receive competent medical attention. The key is that the leader needs the help to deal with EGR people.

Believers Become Disciples of Christ

In traditional churches, Christians easily become preoccupied with secondary issues. They often push agendas on their church that neglect the goal of replicating faith.

The church of the future will challenge people to accept, as its primary agenda for spiritual formation, disciple making through a rich environment of nurturing care. The process involves forming an intentional community, developing leadership, helping people be formed in the image of Christ, and then repeating the cycle until the Lord returns.

True, cell groups need corporate worship and the sense of significance that arises from being part of a churchwide celebration. The leader not only says, "Come," but also guides cell members to attend large-group gatherings of worship to God.

Responsible Christianity embodies more than worship, however. It demands participation in a disciple-making, nurturing cell. This perspective will redefine many believers' expectation of their faith. But it also will challenge and equip them to be *all* they can be for God.

8
Do Away With Malnourishment

Trim the mold off a bar of cheese, and a mouse can have a feast. Remove the pollutants from a system of mouse-size small groups, and each participant will enjoy a banquet of caring nourishment.

What are these contaminants? A host of attitudes and practices that blemish the health of cell ministry. Who causes them? Every still-maturing sinner involved! Impediments to small-group vitality can arise from the membership, the lay leaders, the pastoral staff, and those who've set up caring systems in the church's past.

Using these categories of people, this chapter will explain how seventeen common obstacles to the health of a cell ministry can be detected and overcome.

Warning Signals From Members

1. Lack of Awareness. Most churches can identify a handful of their parishioners who are enmeshed in a strong web of relationships in the church and community. Because these people gain a great amount of support from such friendships, they don't feel a personal need for the alliances that small groups can engender. They might even use their considerable influence to prevent cell ministry from spreading. As these men and women discover that other people lack similar long-standing connections, they'll be more likely to allow a small-group system to go forward.

2. Inflexibility. Some members seem to anchor their spiritual lives on age-old church programs that they know and trust. They respect the values represented by conventional ways of doing things and may oppose attempts to eliminate or repurpose existing ministries. If these traditionalists learn to visualize the needs not merely of themselves, but of others—seekers, newcomers, and their church's lay leadership—they'll begin to allow the Holy Spirit greater freedom in the kinds of ministries He may use.

3. Fear of Intimacy. Many long-term church members feel uncomfortable with the emotions of intimacy and sharing that take place in a well-functioning family or a well-managed small group. As a result, they prefer less personal, middle-sized group fellowships, even if the programs are irrelevant to newcomers. Should these church members develop a friendship with intimate accountability or witness one among their acquaintance network, they'll probably voice greater support for the vision small groups hope to achieve.

4. Prior Biases. Every church experiences a degree of growth as Christians transfer in from other fellowships. Often these relocating believers bring along perceptions of church life that undervalue small groups as caring units or as places where disciples are made. As these newcomers receive teaching in how God uses cells to change lives, their own attitudes may soften and shift.

5. Misguided Expectations. Certain long-standing members have been trained, sometimes for generations, to expect care only from the ordained minister. They overlook the rich resources the Holy Spirit places within the one-another ministry of small groups. Over a long period, many of these people can be reeducated. In the meantime, however, their misguided care requirements needn't impede the shepherding of new members, who aren't nearly so stuck in their perceptions of where spiritual nourishment ought to originate.

6. Bad Memories. Some people have had an unfortunate experience in a group where the lay leader was neither growing nor properly trained. As a result the cell stagnated or possibly died. Such distasteful memories can discourage people, and they become unwilling to give groups a second try. If they can observe and hear testimonies about other capable leaders, however, their stereotypes and disappointments can mellow.

7. Imbalanced Perspective. A few people have had previous experiences with the kind of church cell that admitted no newcomers and elevated the teaching of content over the nurturing of relationships. Consequently, these gatherings didn't allow for sharing, expanding, birthing new groups, or providing intimate care. People with these backgrounds may gradually realize that their prior model had weaknesses and that the Meta-Church paradigm is a far more viable ideal.

8. Lack of Contacts. Some small-group members fear that they won't find enough recruits to enlarge their small group. Usually such people have dwelled for years within the walls of Christendom and have confined their relationships to church members. With no outside friends whom they know well enough to invite, they often look to the minister to draw visitors to church and to Christ, and they spread criticism of their leadership if this doesn't happen.

The solution is patterned after the sea gull who breaks open a mussel shell by lifting it up a hundred feet and then dropping it to the pavement below. These people's tightly encased world calls for an equally dramatic shifting before it will open. Only through this kind of personal crisis or significant spiritual renewal will they understand how God has wanted to invade their tenaciously closed life and church in a way they have not previously experienced.

9. Fear of Loss. Finally, some church people have developed close relationships that were slow and difficult to establish. These people lack confidence that they can form additional or new friendships, and they fear the loss of what they have. Therefore, they don't want their group to grow, lest it divide and their confidants move on. At present, their imaginations lack the hope that replacement companions will be available.

Warning Signals From Lay Leaders

The above nine barriers to a healthy cell ministry stem largely from blockages created by church members. What about the lay leaders of a small group? What impediments might they create? This section details the four most typical situations.

1. Ministry Fatigue. In every church, a certain number of lay leaders have taken on too many commitments and are prime candidates for ministry burnout. Their necks ache from wearing too many hats— choir president, bowling team coordinator, nursery substitute, chauffeur for elderly Grandma Carol, Sunday-morning greeter, youth sponsor, and cell-group pastor!

Some have contracted a case of terminal fatigue and will soon move on to the anonymity of a different and usually larger church. Others will stay and heal, but only if they deal with a couple of possible infections: biting off more than they can chew, rather than doing just a few things well, and insisting that only they can handle certain church jobs, rather than relinquishing their power controls to others.

2. Unrealistic Goals. Even if lay leaders limit their number of commitments, they invite frustration when they allow their cell group to outgrow its span-of-care capabilities. It's like the time the George family's eight-nippled championship golden retriever bore a litter of thirteen pups; my wife and I realized we had to provide backup nursing via syringe, or someone was going to starve.

Similarly, some cell leaders will congregate fifteen or more people into a weekly home meeting. That overextended span of care inevitably leads to unhappy group members: Nobody can listen to their stories, because too many people are clamoring for attention! To make matters worse, the sort of layperson who takes on this load is often the kind who wears all the hats: facilitator, hospitality host, recruiter, and teacher. Unless the cell leader receives regular guidance from the pastoral staff, he or she will one day just give up and quit.

3. Lack of Referral. Many laypeople have led groups where a misbehaving member destroyed the experience for everyone. This EGR person ("extra grace required"—*see* Chapter 7) seems to have a hole in his or her soul. Although an entire group pours in all the love they can find, an EGR will still complain, blame, and demand more. No matter how much acceptance small groups show, EGRs will use the gathering as an explosive courtroom-style hearing to play out their hurt and sickness, rather than to find healing.

Leaders who've watched helplessly as an EGR spoiled their group often lose their nerve, feeling that they won't know how to manage this kind of person in the future. These leaders need to be coached, something that probably didn't happen in their previous experiences. They haven't yet learned that the love of Christ involves sending EGRs to a place where they can get help, instead of keeping them where they cause harm. Leaders also need to be counseled in how to send such people for therapy (ideally, to a church-sponsored support and recovery group) or how to ask them to leave the group. Otherwise, the leader is allowing the Body of Christ in that cell to be sick.

4. Lack of Foresight. Some leaders become stuck. They haven't recruited anyone to replace themselves. The reason, in part, is that no one guided them to develop an apprentice. At some point they'll want a break, but instead they'll stay at the helm in order to keep the ministry going. At the next available opportunity, they'll refuse to reenlist, fearing entrapment again in the same circumstances. The memory of this bad experience will prevent them from putting their hearts into small-group ministry.

Warning Signals From Pastors

The pastor's role in leadership training and cell-group management is so important that Chapters 9 and 11 focus on those topics. Three pastor-related cautions are best described here, as they affect not only the lay leaders, but the tenor of the entire church as well.

1. Fear of Division. Pastors fear schism and false doctrine. Part of a shepherd's job is to guard the sheep, knowing that ". . . Savage wolves will come in among you and will not spare the flock. Even from your own number men will arise and distort the truth in order to draw away disciples after them" (Acts 20:29, 30).

Many small groups have leaders who disseminate doctrines opposed to the teachings and emphases of their churches. Even worse, while it's uncommon to hear of a Sunday-school class leaving a church en masse, any minister who has worked for long with small groups can relate a horror story of a home-based group that joined another church and became a power center of gossip and divisive discussions.

Cell groups, like all other forms of ministry, involve risks. They open doors to possible damage. If, however, pastors properly manage their cell groups through monitoring, teaching, and providing curriculum resources, the gains will far outnumber the losses.

2. Jealousy. Pastors sometimes fear the loss of exclusive authority in matters of guidance and advice. Each of Christendom's traditions contains certain finer points of doctrine or practice that allow for multiple interpretation options. Some pastors have a need to be right and to be in control, lest their competence seem challenged or threatened. This kind of minister will experience difficulty in multiplying teachers, advisors, counselors, and other persons of wisdom, since these lay pastors may come to wield almost as much influence in their small groups as their senior pastor.

Similarly, some pastors become wounded or jealous when their lay ministers receive the affirmation that used to be reserved for the professional minister. As the number of church cells multiplies and the span of care touches far more people than even a superclergy could reach, these grateful people will naturally stroke their most immediate point of contact: their cell-group leader. These small group participants may overlook the fact that the senior pastor—who sometimes has a thin skin—is the one responsible for making the help available!

3. Lack of Confidence or Training. Many pastors don't believe they have the skills to motivate their group leaders with the vision that cell ministry is worthwhile.

North America's first church to cross the 15,000 attendance level did so largely because Pastor Jack Hyles could connect with his bus drivers in a way that they caught the dream: "The best use of a Saturday is knocking on doors so that, one bus seat at a time, I can reach boys and girls for Christ."

Likewise, missionary promoters can be used of God to inspire affluent North American young people to dedicate their lives to the people of some shantytown slum. These youth grasp the idea that one person can make an incredible difference.

But how many pastors have a well-developed vision-casting ability that inspires lay leaders to conclude, *I want to invest myself in pastoring ten people*?

This lack of confidence can seriously impede the development of a small-group ministry. In reality, most ministers possess the ability, but they've not learned how to apply it.

What, for example, is one of the most successful worship services in most churches? Mother's Day, when the minister delivers a sugar-stick sermon to extol the role of the family nurturer, mother. Why not hitchhike on that event to acclaim the significance of being a spiritual nurturer to a spiritual kinship group? Most ministers could; they're simply not used to thinking that way.

For many people, the small-group leader offers the only living touch of God that can reach the root of their dysfunctional family life, current relationships, and scars from the past. If a privilege like that doesn't provide meaning and significance to a lay leader, nothing can!

Warning Signals From the Past

Almost every page of Scripture douses the reader with the importance of loving, caring, and nurturing. Consequently, most churches have experimented with programs and systems designed to facilitate these qualities.

The following material examines the predominant ways churches seek to provide care. It then suggests that metagrowth theory, designed to discover and avoid the deficiencies of traditional practice, is the system that will dominate numerically flourishing churches of the future. With the promise of superseding every system of care developed to date, the Meta-Church is the most effective way to reach today's harvest and make disciples of Christ.

Clergy- and Para-Clergy-Based Care. The most prevalent system of pastoral care is what pastors themselves typically provide. First, they're on twenty-four-hour call for hospital and family crises. Then, on Sundays, they make themselves available after the services. In addition, they provide one-on-one counseling, although my interviews point to eleven hours a week with at most eleven people as the maximum they can handle without sacrificing their other responsibilities. In fact, were it not for people who drop by their offices unexpectedly or phone them at home over the dinner hour, most clergy couldn't invest even those eleven hours.

Ministers soon reach a saturation point where they can't handle additional demands. Every people situation seems to scream for first aid or surgery. The pastor struggles to keep up, commonly running out of hours long before running out of people to see. This human limitation explains why the usual pastor is more comfortable with a church of 75 than of 200—unless this larger flock is trouble free, due to living in a "village" (see Chapter 5) where mothers and "mayors" take care of most issues.

Pastors also try to do visitation. Nowadays unannounced home calls still work in certain blue-collar and ethnic communities, but visitation by appointment requires commitment of huge blocks of time. Plus, if it is compared to a direct-face sales call in the business community, each personal engagement costs hundreds of dollars apiece!

Most people in middle-class America and Canada prefer phone visitation, because it's less of a burden. But most pastors have difficulty organizing themselves to use the telephone systematically and strategically.

Finally, pastors sometimes build pastoral rapport through the mail, using notes, letters, photocopied articles, and cassette tapes. This tool helps, but it, too, has a limited scope and depth.

The only remaining option is for the number of workers to be multiplied. For that to happen, the pastor needs some sort of strategy and plan.

One of the best specialized approaches at copying the caring portfolio of a pastor is the Stephen Ministries training established by Lutheran clinical psychologist Kenneth Haugk of St. Louis, Missouri. A pastor sends parishioners for training in certain skills and then refers crisis-care situations to them. Stephen Ministries training for lay leaders exceeds in quality the training many ordained clergy have received!

This helpful system cannot avoid a long-range problem, however: It clones the same organizational system that bred the problems to begin with. Stephen Ministries operates largely on a para-clergy model.

By contrast, the most therapeutic pastoral support comes from being part of a social unit, a nurturing cell group that accepts, guides, sticks with, and confronts a person as would a healthy extended family. That's what the Meta-Church idea, with its multiplication of lay-pastor-led cells, is all about. Therefore, the greatest effectiveness of Stephen Ministries comes when its skill training is used to equip small group leaders.

Deacon Ministries. The second most common strategy for congregational care, after the pastor, is deacon ministry. While not all churches establish an office of deacon, many have built equivalent lay caring systems. Whatever title the structure receives, it will probably contain a similar series of infirmities.

Typically, deacons divide the church membership into geographic or ZIP code groups of between fifteen and thirty households. The church computer picks out the appropriate lists, and each deacon receives simple instructions: "See to it that these people are cared for."

Soon the ministry fails, and the deacons start asking themselves why. Sometimes they decide the assignment was impractical because of its size. So they recruit and supervise Yokefellows ("I ask you, loyal yokefellow, help" other believers. [Philippians 4:3]). That strategy creates a larger core of deacon-type laborers, but the assistant-deacon Yokefellows often feel too remote from the church staff and too untrained to deliver the kind of care needed.

The initial problem lies in the faulty assumptions behind using a ZIP code type of system. People rarely develop relationships based on whose house is nearby. Churchgoers may be aware of other parishioners who live in their neighborhood, but commonly have no connection beyond an occasional, "We're staying for a meeting—do you mind dropping our Johnny off on the way home?" Thus the geographical proximity of living in a particular deacon's quadrant adds little to someone's receptivity to ministry.

Instead, friendships and ministry relationships grow on the basis of three factors. First, how do people's life paths bring them across the paths of others? These travel patterns surface both at church, such as where people park or like to sit, as well as in natural contacts through their social world or worlds. The deacon who attends the second service and sits in the far corner may never see the family who lives down the street and catches the early service from the front pew.

Second, what kind of social match do people's life-styles hold in common? Variables include recreational interests, preferences in clothing, glamour consciousness, and how they maintain their homes. A church member and a deacon may dwell on the same block, but if the member boasts a manicured lawn and the deacon a graveyard of every family car for the last twenty years, these two people may have a hard time merely staying on speaking terms!

Third, and most important, people need opportunity for affinity declarations. Whom would they pick as their caregiver? Which fellow parishioners do they already respect and trust? Whom would they like to get to know and be with? Assignment by third party, whatever the system, tends not to work well.

Deacon flock ministries also experience problems in their reporting systems. Deacons, with so many to care for, cannot maintain close enough touch to learn of crises and needs as they are developing. Our society has lost its across-the-back-fence network of women at home who phone and talk with one another. Nor can answering machines replace that method of polling the fellowship. Sunday attendance records do not always help. A deacon can call a parishioner whom the friendship pad indicated was absent, only to get a false response ("I forgot to sign it") or a rebuke ("Oh, we changed churches several months ago"). As a result, deacons lose confidence in the system and are demotivated for staying in touch.

The other major shortfall in deacon ministry involves inconsistencies in training and supervision. Deacons may meet monthly, but they receive no pastoral monitoring other than a notebook or job description as they come into office. It would appear that many ministers, when their deacon board becomes lax and ineffective, simply pray and wait for the next elections!

Most deacons genuinely want to be more capable shepherds, but don't know how. Many of those who experience success are found to be treating their charges as a group whom they invite over for dessert, conversation, a devotional thought from Scripture, and prayer. Even though such meetings are only monthly or quarterly, these effective deacons typically are men who have wives who don't work outside the home and who therefore can spend much time on the phone networking with church people!

When I suggest to the pastors that deacon-and-people gatherings become official small groups, they say, "Surely you don't want me to require deacons to hold cell-group meetings on top of everything else we have them doing?" I then question why the deacons couldn't give up everything else. "That won't work either. There's too much for them to do!"

At this point I agree. The reason seems straightforward: Deacons are being kept too busy to minister! (*See* Chapter 6's discussion of tele-care's crisis response teams for an example of how deacon energies might be redeployed.)

Sunday School. A third widespread care system is the Sunday school. This organization, founded two centuries ago to improve literacy among England's mill village children, has developed historically through a number of stages. The advent of a public-education system, of publishing houses for religious curriculum, of church buildings with wraparound, cubicle-shaped classrooms, and of professional Christian-education directors, have shaped a Sunday school mind-set that tends to focus more on instruction than on care. This shift of perspective affects both adult and children's Sunday school.

The more effective Sunday schools have refused to succumb to lesson-centered content orientation. These churches work hard to be pupil-focused centers of care that stress obedience more than knowledge. They provide a sense of neighborhood community, friendships, and wholesome nurture that resembles the small-town sidewalk paintings of the late artist Norman Rockwell. This is consistent with the village analogy developed in Chapter 5. This kind of heartwarming Sunday school is ideal for suburbia, where a sense of neighborhood stability exists and where healthy nuclear families march the kids to church for catechism. Where's the inadequacy, then? In healthy churches, the problem lies with the future: This previously helpful Sunday-school formula is becoming increasingly obsolete. Churches today, especially metropolitan ones, increasingly will lack the funds or the available land to construct the kind of facilities formerly used to make Sunday school a useful tool. Church leaders need innovations that will allow us to take adult Christian education back to the home and neighborhood.

Some church Sunday schools have already experienced an erosion of the care and obedience factors. The curriculum orientation produces an imbalance of cognitive learning. The formalism of a classroom seems too removed from adult life. The on-premises location gives a higher degree of control to the church staff than to the teacher. And the educational setting constrains the comfortable social feel that would be achieved in a home as friends linger afterwards, sitting in soft chairs and interacting freely.

Sunday schools are experimenting with a number of factors that might fix this dilemma: care directors and hospitality coordinators for adult classes, breakout cell groups for teenagers, Christian "Sesame Street" style programs for extended children's church times, interest-center approaches for preschoolers, and intergenerational Sunday school for parents to gain skills in relating to their children.

But the new church lacks the budget and the pastoral staff to direct this kind of ministry. And many established churches can't get teachers to commit for long enough terms to maintain these programs.

I affirm all the advantages of our current models of Sunday school, as well as the indispensableness of churches providing something on premises for children during adult worship. But I anticipate that the wave of the future will bring sweeping changes. The format must fit today's society. And the orientation must focus on care and obedience to the Word of God.

I believe that the care system to supplement and eventually supersede Sunday school in priority will be the lay-pastor-led nurture group. (*See* further comments about the Sunday school in Chapter 10.)

The Meta-Church calls for a new way of thinking and a new style of ministry. It must, as Chapter 4 emphasized, start with the pastor and then impact every area of a church.

Meta-Church principles lose strength if diluted by being added to existing programs. But if implemented properly, such a church, which is based on a small-group experience that covers the entire membership, will provide a solid foundation for disciple making in the next generation—and for millennia.

9
Train Your Leaders Thoroughly

When our children were young, my wife and I enrolled them in a soccer club. The experience taught me an excellent lesson about the priorities involved in pastoring a church.

The soccer association fit together over five distinct roles: the numerous color-coordinated teams of players; the whistle-blowing referees; the coaches, who paced the sidelines; the parents, who milled around and cheered; and the director, who ensured that the whole operation came together.

I rarely saw the director, yet his influence affected every person and shaped every aspect of the soccer organization. He delivered a motivational sermon at the children's sign-up meeting; he led the coaches' clinic (I dropped out because I couldn't meet the requirement to be present at every game, and they didn't know that shared roles or cocoaching was an option); he observed a few of our games; and he spoke at the awards banquet at the end of the season.

This man embodied the training and experience necessary to be a player, coach, referee, parent, or director. But had he tried to do all these activities at the same level of priority, he would have failed. He would get the uniforms ready and review a dispute over a ground rule, but in the process he could not neglect the more important issue: overseeing the training of his coaches so that they, in turn, could keep encouraging their team members. The soccer association would not prosper unless the key leader prioritized this most important activity.

The same dynamics govern a church. Every local fellowship consists of many specific roles that not even Reverend Multi-Gift can fill singlehandedly. A minister who wants to experience a championship season must come to view every group leader as a team coach and every parishioner as a potential player. Otherwise, the pastor will become so wrapped up in all the other tasks that the most important one slips: the developing of lay cell-group leaders.

Pastors act as players when they preach, visit at hospital bedsides, counsel, and in dozens of other ways offer primary care. When all their time and energy go into that player role, they lose sight of the significance of directing. If they won't make time to work on the management of the church as a whole, their ministry can't expand.

Pastors must realize the necessity of lay persons who act as team leaders—the equivalent of soccer-team coaches. They must rearrange their ministry around the concept that God doesn't want the clergy to do everything themselves; He counts on the laity to do it (Ephesians 4:11–13). The best way to mobilize entire teams of laypeople is for each pastor to train groups of team leaders. As pastors gain this global view of their people and ministries, they won't get lost trying to be players when they should be directing.

I'm convinced that the larger part of ministry needs to take place in a familylike atmosphere of a small-group meeting in a home. As "coaches" guide "players" to use the Holy Spirit's gifts of wisdom, teaching, encouragement, loving, confrontation, and rebuke, believers will speak truth in love, and disciples will be built.

The pastor, as director, represents the pivotal link in outfitting coaches for their vital role. Leadership development is so essential that Meta-Churches cannot leave it to chance. The pastor establishes and manages a finely tuned system of linkages between supervisors and coaches, resulting in the ongoing creation of effective church leadership.

The purpose of this chapter is to explain the equipping process that takes place between pastor and cell leader. Chapter 11 will address the dynamics between pastor and the rest of the church staff.

A Biblical Precedent

Some time ago, I spent six months reading and meditating on Exodus 18. In the chapter, especially vv. 13–23, Moses' father-in-law, Jethro, offers a wise alternative to Moses' one-man court system. Israel was so sizeable (Exodus 12:37) that judicial needs were bottle-necking. People ". . . stood around him from morning till evening" (v. 13), waiting for Moses' care.

" '. . . The work is too heavy for you; you cannot handle it alone,' " Jethro observed (v. 18). Possibly from military practice of the day (Numbers 31:4), he suggested a decentralized appellate system. It would enable Moses to " 'stand the strain' " and the people to " 'go home satisfied' " (v. 23). Using levels of tens, fifties, hundreds, and thousands, Jethro organized the tribes, in effect, on a series of neighborhood, municipal, state, and national courts. He decentralized the meting out of justice to the lowest level possible.

The system started with the family as the basic building block and grouped households by tens under a local leader. This approach enabled each group to engage in conflict resolution within a suitable span of control.

If the issues raised fit within standard operating procedure, which most did, they could be resolved and promptly quieted there at that first level. After a while, most problems could be solved through case law and routine, and thus fewer people would need the courts.

Any complaints and circumstances that didn't fit the routine would go to the next adjudication and, if necessary, to each successively higher level. This system of management by exception permitted only a few cases to reach Moses. These toughest issues hadn't been settled somewhere else. Moses was able to sleep, think, and make a trip to Mount Sinai for a word from God that would establish a new precedent in Israel's law.

While the purpose of Jethro's judicial model was to manage complaints and exceptions, it also regularized the nation. The orderly system of progressive legal precedents brought about a stability that could continue if Moses were to die and a new leader succeed him.

What if all the roles weren't filled? What if, like an army whose officer group is hit with casualties, certain gaps appeared? The system could still function, because it contained slightly more leadership than required. As military parlance would describe it, Israel had redundancy of organization.

Notice, for example, that nowhere in the structure does the span of control exceed a ratio of one to ten. If we use symbols from the Roman-numeral system (I=one, X=ten, L=fifty, C=a hundred, and M=a thousand), the X leader at the foundational level handles the legal complaints of *ten* households (or ten I's).

At the next level, the span of control drops as one L oversees *five* X's. The next level reduces further to one C overseeing only *two* L's. The final level goes back up to one M over *ten* C's. (*See* Chart 9.)

Suppose an overload develops, such as an L (a captain of fifty) becoming disabled. How does that affect span of control for the C (the leader of a hundred)? Instead of overseeing just two people (the pair of L's) the C must manage six people (the remaining L and the five X's). Six people is a small enough group that the C has enough breathing room to locate, cultivate, and train another L.

Adaptation to Today

Can Jethro's court system, with its workable spans of control, be adapted to church administration, with its need for feasible spans of care? Could Jethro, who dared to offer ecclesiastical advice to his son-in-law and who was a priest himself (Exodus 18:1, 11), model today's church-growth consultant? I think so. We'll call the modification Jethro II.

Let's liken a cell group to ten I's (individuals) and its lay leader to an X. Most of the X's will represent one-another nurture groups, although a few task groups will be included as well. (Chapter 6 introduced these types of groups.)

The lay coach who trains five X's is the L. In smaller churches and churches just starting cell ministry, pastors may function as the L's. But in order for the number of cells to keep multiplying, laypeople will be cultivated as L's as soon as possible.

Jethro II, for Cell Group Leaders

D=Staff
L=Coach
X=Cell Group
Leader

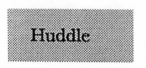

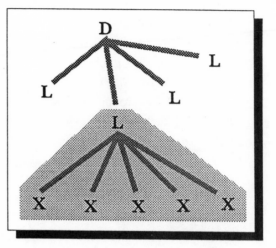

Jethro II, With Apprentices Shown

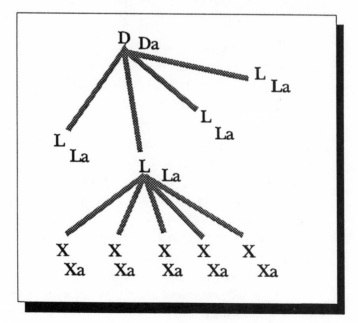

Chart 9

As part of accommodating the shift from court system to church system, we'll label the next person not as a C (leader of 100) but as a D (the Roman numeral for 500). This D, responsible for up to ten L's, will be a member of the full-time pastoral staff. Therefore we'll not use the letter M; the Jethro II system goes no higher than one or more D's. (*See* Chart 9.)

Are there any C's? Yes, in larger churches. The C's manage any congregation-size groups the church may have, such as adult Bible fellowships, departmental assemblies, singles' ministries or senior adult programs. Each D oversees up to five C's, along with up to ten L's.

The C's and the L's run on separate accountability tracks, however, lest they compete with each other. They interact in only two ways. First they see each other at the leadership meeting, which involves all D's, C's, L's, X's, and sometimes apprentices. Second, the C's allow their congregation-size groups to serve as "fishing pools" for the L's and X's with their apprentices to meet and recruit potential cell-group members. The C's even plan specific times of acquaintance-facilitating foursomes so that X's and apprentices can have opportunities to build new relationships.

Is it healthy for the D's span of care to exceed the one-to-ten ratio? This higher proportion can work only under certain conditions. First, the D, being full-time and mobile, will need to spend thirty to forty hours a week in visitation. His or her C's must be stable and mature enough that the D–C supervisory meetings can be collective ones for planning purposes. Further, most of the L's in a Meta-Church will oversee *nurture* groups; the more *task* forces with varying agendas represented, the fewer L's one person can supervise. Finally, the D must have clerical or secretarial assistance and, if possible, a lay understudy (Da) as well.

A final dynamic: One goal of the Meta-Church is to retain as many extra group leaders as possible. The more trained leadership present, the more a church can grow. Historically, for every Sunday-school teacher or small-group leader commissioned, a church's attendance average increased by seven to ten.

Therefore each D, C, L, and X will want to develop an apprentice. These understudies will be designated Da, Ca, La, and Xa. Secretarial help, such as for the D and Da, though indispensable, doesn't receive its own Roman numeral in this Jethro II system. (*See* Chart 9.)

Why Groups of Ten or Fewer?

Notice that in adapting Jethro's span-of-control model to a Jethro II church setting, I'm maintaining the span-of-care limit of ten people maximum. The Flake Formula, described in Chapter 2, confirms experientially that this number works best, but we must turn to the behavioral sciences for an insight as to why.

The key to the architecture of care is the activity called listening. People don't feel cared for until someone has heard them. Person A develops loyalty to Person B in direct proportion to how well Person B gives attention to what Person A is communicating or trying to say.

I may observe, for example, a problem situation in the church I attend. If I complain and someone listens, then I will feel valued and can continue to be loyal to that person. In addition, my sense of ownership will increase. If, by contrast, I complain, and the organization is unresponsive and refuses to receive the message, then my anxiety increases. I can yell louder, start slamming doors, or if I'm aggravated enough, leave. Most people depart quietly, but others make their exit with a great door slam.

No one can listen to a hundred voices at once. Most leaders have a hard enough time keeping track of ten without the flock starting to feel uncared for. Further, just as Jethro's judges were unsalaried locals who did their work when they could, out of their shepherding time, so church lay workers can handle only so much span of care before they themselves burn out. For these reasons, small groups that grow beyond ten need to divide.

In fact, research suggests that ten people is usually too great a number for one person to nurture. Consider the mathematics of communication. In a group of two, the interplay involves two exchanges: what you are signaling to Person B, and what Person B is signaling back to you.

Add a Person C to that loop, and the number of transactions rises to nine (you're monitoring each of them; they're each monitoring you; they're monitoring each other; and you're monitoring their interaction with each other).

If a fourth person comes in, the signal count jumps to twenty-eight. Why? In addition to monitoring your response to each of the other three and vice versa, you must also observe them in groups of two and three—and they must do the same with one another!

For example, Person A's suggestion produces a "good idea" grin from Person B, who is at the same time signaling acute nervousnesses by drumming his fingers. Yet Person A's suggestion also draws a "Let's talk more" scowl from Person C, who scribbles *Forget it* on the back of her note pad, which only Person D can see!

With the addition of a fifth person, the number of permutations mounts to seventy-five. By this point, much goes unnoticed by even the most alert facilitators. Remember, the issue is that people are listened to and responded to.

In a ten-person group the number of interpersonal signals to detect exceeds 5,000! (*See* Chart 10.) Thus some churches, including some of the beyond-huge ones in Korea, feel that even ten is too large.

Another partial solution, the one I implied in Chapter 7's description of cell leadership, is for each group of ten to involve an apprentice leader (designated as an Xa). Two leaders (an X and an Xa) in a ten-person group reduces the span of care to a ratio of one to four.

Thus, the typical nurture group will contain an X (the facilitating leader), an Xa (the apprentice leader), and several people described in Chapter 7, who can now be given symbols: H (the hospitality host), G's (growing Christians), S's (seekers), EGR (an "extra grace required" person who may need to be referred to a healing group), E (person who will next fill the empty chair), and L (the coach of the X's, who occasionally visits to observe). (*See* Chart 11.)

If quality care giving entails so many small-group dynamics, then does anything significant occur at the middle-size congregational or much larger celebrational level? Certainly—all kinds of essential activities! (*See* the celebration-congregation-cell comparison chart in Chapter 5.) Some large-size ministries project a charisma of symbolic care as one person—such as a pastor or Sunday-school teacher—holds out and the others respond, experiencing warmth, much as audiences do in the presence of skilled performers. But primary nurturative

Signal Counts in Small Groups

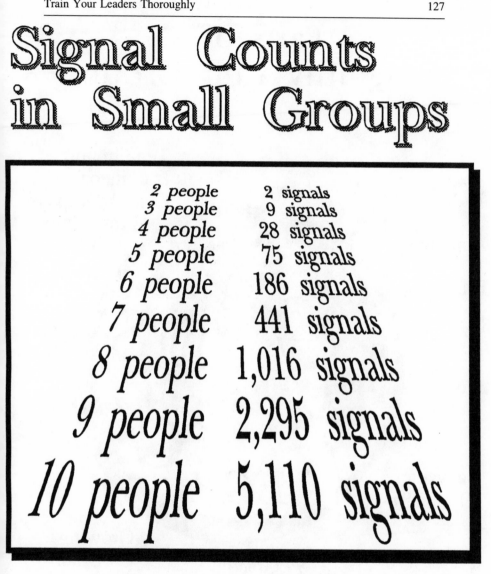

2 people	2 signals
3 people	9 signals
4 people	28 signals
5 people	75 signals
6 people	186 signals
7 people	441 signals
8 people	1,016 signals
9 people	2,295 signals
10 people	5,110 signals

from Human Scale by Kirkpatrick Sale

Chart 10

Parts of a
Healthy Cell Group

Ten-Group Facilitator

Ten-Group
Facilitator's
Coach (Drops by
From Time
to Time)

Apprentice
Ten-Group
Facilitator

Seeker

Host/
Hostess

Empty
Chair

Babysitter
(Optional)

Growing
Christian

Extra Grace
Required
Person
(Also Optional,
but Expected)

Chart 11

care—mutual care of peers encouraging and serving one another—
requires a cell-level context.

Who Are These Leaders?

Which book in the New Testament, some will ask, proposes such
titles as D, C, L, X, and I? Won't a biblical model instead speak of
bishops, pastors, elders, and deacons? Plus, don't certain texts (1
Timothy 2, 3; Titus 1–2; 1 Corinthians 12–14; and so on) imply age-
and gender-based qualifications?

First, I'm not suggesting that we tamper with the precedents of
Scripture. Nor do I advocate tossing out the honorific titles churches
give to recognize someone's loyalty or exemplary life-style: be it *class
president, trustee emeritus,* or whatever.

What concerns me is the baggage that accompanies these positions—
all the ideas we think come from Scripture but really don't! Certain
traditions and imbalanced emphases account for many churches' lack
of more rapid expansion. In short, too often those people who are
"supposed to" care don't, and the people who aren't officially en-
trusted with caring do.

One of the strengths of Meta-Church theory is its biblical conviction
that the Holy Spirit officially commissions *every* believer into a ministry of caring for one another. After all, *none* of the following commands are restricted to a particular title (such as elders only) or a
particular gender (such as men only).

The "One Anothers" of the New Testament[1]

1. ". . . Be at peace with each other" (Mark 9:50).
2. ". . . Wash one another's feet" (John 13:14).
3. ". . . Love one another . . ." (John 13:34).
4. ". . . Love one another" (John 13:34).
5. ". . . Love one another" (John 13:35).
6. ". . . Love each other . . ." (John 15:12).
7. ". . . Love each other" (John 15:17).
8. "Be devoted to one another in brotherly love . . ."
   (Romans 12:10).
9. ". . . Honor one another above yourselves" (Romans
   12:10).
10. "Live in harmony with one another . . ." (Romans 12:16).

11. ". . . Love one another . . ." (Romans 13:8).
12. ". . . Stop passing judgment on one another" (Romans 14:13).
13. "Accept one another, then, just as Christ accepted you . . ." (Romans 15:7).
14. ". . . Instruct one another" (Romans 15:14).
15. "Greet one another with a holy kiss . . ." (Romans 16:16).
16. ". . . When you come together to eat, wait for each other" (1 Corinthians 11:33).
17. ". . . Have equal concern for each other" (1 Corinthians 12:25).
18. ". . . Greet one another with a holy kiss" (1 Corinthians 16:20).
19. "Greet one another with a holy kiss" (2 Corinthians 13:12).
20. ". . . Serve one another in love" (Galatians 5:13).
21. "If you keep on biting and devouring each other . . . you will be destroyed by each other" (Galatians 5:15).
22. "Let us not become conceited, provoking and envying each other" (Galatians 5:26).
23. "Carry each other's burdens . . ." (Galatians 6:2).
24. ". . . Be patient, bearing with one another in love" (Ephesians 4:2).
25. "Be kind and compassionate to one another . . ." (Ephesians 4:32).
26. ". . . Forgiving each other . . ." (Ephesians 4:32).
27. "Speak to one another with psalms, hymns and spiritual songs" (Ephesians 5:19).
28. "Submit to one another out of reverence for Christ" (Ephesians 5:21).
29. ". . . In humility consider others better than yourselves" (Philippians 2:3).
30. "Do not lie to each other . . ." (Colossians 3:9).
31. "Bear with each other . . ." (Colossians 3:13).
32. ". . . Forgive whatever grievances you may have against one another" (Colossians 3:13).
33. "Teach . . . [one another]" (Colossians 3:16).
34. ". . . Admonish one another" (Colossians 3:16).
35. ". . . Make your love increase and overflow for each other" (1 Thessalonians 3:12).
36. ". . . Love each other" (1 Thessalonians 4:9).

37. ". . . Encourage each other . . ." (1 Thessalonians 4:18).
38. ". . . Encourage one another . . ." (1 Thessalonians 5:11).
39. ". . . Build each other up . . ." (1 Thessalonians 5:11).
40. "Encourage one another daily . . ." (Hebrews 3:13).
41. ". . . Spur one another on toward love and good deeds" (Hebrews 10:24).
42. ". . . Encourage one another" (Hebrews 10:25).
43. ". . . Do not slander one another" (James 4:11).
44. "Don't grumble against each other . . ." (James 5:9).
45. "Confess your sins to each other . . ." (James 5:16).
46. ". . . Pray for each other" (James 5:16).
47. ". . . Love one another deeply, from the heart" (1 Peter 1:22).
48. ". . . Live in harmony with one another . . ." (1 Peter 3:8).
49. ". . . Love each other deeply . . ." (1 Peter 4:8).
50. "Offer hospitality to one another without grumbling" (1 Peter 4:9).
51. "Each one should use whatever gift he has received to serve others . . ." (1 Peter 4:10).
52. ". . . Clothe yourselves with humility toward one another . . ." (1 Peter 5:5).
53. "Greet one another with a kiss of love" (1 Peter 5:14).
54. ". . . Love one another" (1 John 3:11).
55. ". . . Love one another . . ." (1 John 3:23).
56. ". . . Love one another . . ." (1 John 4:7).
57. ". . . Love one another . . ." (1 John 4:11).
58. ". . . Love one another . . ." (1 John 4:12).
59. ". . . Love one another" (2 John 5).

Twenty-one of the fifty-nine, or fully one third, call for Christians to *love!*

Scores of additional passages enjoin *all* believers to love their neighbors as themselves, build up the church, be involved in mutual edification, be like-minded, be of one accord, and similarly ". . . do good . . . to those who belong to the family of believers" (Galatians 6:10).

Add to these commands the many other Scriptures that describe the role of caring. One Bible writer, for instance, marvels at how Christ's forgiveness gives rise to true ". . . fellowship with one another . . ." (1 John 1:7). Another thanks God for the maturity whereby ". . . the love every one of you has for each other is increasing" (2 Thessalonians 1:3).

I suggest that churches will make maximum progress toward the future if they unlink traditional roles from metacell nurture. We must distinguish between formal enrollment in office (the elder board that governs the church) and lay ministry (people who facilitate one-another caring).

By doing so, the pool of potential caregivers will remain as large as possible. Otherwise, as soon as an organizational system correlates titles (*pastor, elder, and deacon*) with cell-group leadership, a lot of God-given talent will go unused. (*See* Chart 12.)

One church staff analyzed the Jethro II system and concluded, "The X's, Xa's, L's, and La's seem closest to what biblical elders ought to be." So they decided that only elders—meaning 2 percent of their membership—could be cell-group leaders, coaches, or apprentices.

They instantly bottlenecked their small-group ministry. Even if all 2 percent who were the elders took active part in small-group leadership, the cells would reach their ten-person maximum when a mere 10 percent of the church had become involved.

Then, until additional elders could be secured to serve as fresh Xa's, no new cells could be birthed. In another church adopting an elder-led cell strategy, they had developed a six-month waiting list before any newcomers could join a small group!

The application? Beware of attempts to link sex roles, title roles, or elected-position roles with Meta-Church roles! Most modern role definitions for church leaders, even though they claim to be biblically derived, tend to be shaped more by the characteristics of the nineteenth-century church than by New Testament teaching.

What, then, to call these people? Many churches use the metajargon's Roman numerals to avoid role-based stereotypes: "Our L's and C's will meet Tuesday night at 7:30"; "I'm an Xa in the cell that Mark Edwards leads"; "My L was just teaching us about that last week!"

WHO CAN DO WHAT?
It is helpful to unlink the various
roles during early implementation

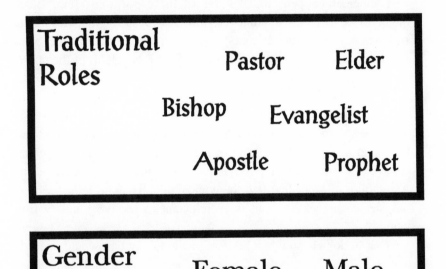

Traditional Roles   Pastor   Elder
                Bishop   Evangelist
                Apostle   Prophet

Gender Roles   Female   Male

Meta-Church Roles   C   CEO   D
                X   La   Ca
                Da   Xa   L

Chart 12

I suggest that for the first few years of a Meta-Church's existence or transition, everybody think in terms of ministry (rather than title), and that all cell-group leadership describe their responsibility as such: "I minister as an X, a leader of ten"; "I serve as an L, a coach of five group leaders." Remember, all disciples are legitimately called to lead others by serving them! (Mark 10:42–45; John 13:12–17; 2 Corinthians 5:17–21).

If an elder happens to take one of these positions, fine. Elders ought to be allowed to minister, too! Maybe cell-group leadership will accomplish more ministry than warming a chair in the board room, as necessary as sitting on a board is to the health of the church body.

Dr. Paul Yonggi Cho, pastor of the world's largest church, ministers in Korea. That culture is akin to our continent in the 1950s, when men dominated the business world and women the home front. He found that 80 to 85 percent of his most effective care-group leaders were women. Even through his denomination at the time, the Assemblies of God, had few theological qualms about letting women minister, many of his men were reluctant to receive ministry from women!

What to do? He sought a biblical methodology that would open the door for this 85 percent of his work force. Noting in 1 Corinthians 11:10 that women could pray or prophesy but needed a sign of authority to do so, he designed a prayer cap, in appearance not unlike a beanie, for each of his female cell-group leaders to wear. After all, even the best Bible commentators aren't certain whether the "covering" described is hair, a veil, a hat, or something else. Maybe it was a beanie like today's Jewish yarmulke!

Then he said, "Women, I'm giving you a covering. You must make reports and teach what I tell you to disseminate. Here's the outline for next week. Now, go minister." Eventually tens of thousands of them did.

Some men, observing mixed-sex groups facilitated by women, objected, saying, "But women shouldn't teach or have authority over men [1 Timothy 2:12]." Pastor Cho answered, "I am the official teacher. They're taking orders from me, so they aren't usurping my authority. And they're wearing coverings. So they pass muster with Saint Paul's rules."

My point is not to argue the issue of women's liberation. Rather, I speak in favor of the advance of the Great Commission. If a church focuses its groups as teaching ministries, some people will have problems with men sitting under women. But if the groups are to encourage the "one anothers" of spiritual life, the gender of the person facilitating the meetings or leading the groups won't matter.

Let's not kick a sacred cow. But let's not assume that every point of our church histories embody the Holy Spirit's wisdom. Very possibly the Spirit of God is opening doors our traditions haven't anticipated. He did that with the deinstitutionalization of slavery, and he might be doing the same with the ministry of women.

How to Develop the Leadership Community

Many Christians have accepted an absolutely stupid notion: that a person can be lectured into leadership. Leader behaviors, by definition, require followers. Leadership formation cannot occur without on-the-job coaching by someone to whom the leadership trainee is willing to be responsible. Speeches on leader traits will never produce the harvest God wants to grant.

The Meta-Church structure for providing leadership training includes meeting with lay leaders and assuring that three functions occur. Sometimes this is called the VHS meeting. We recommend a twice-a-month gathering of D's, Da's, C's, Ca's, L's, La's, X's, and Xa's for a three-deck sandwich: The top layer or function signifies *Vision*, with the storytelling that is appropriate to vision casting; the middle layer is *Huddle*; and the bottom layer is *Skill*. (*See* Chart 13.) Each activity in idealized leadership community meeting takes about forty minutes, for a total of about two hours.

Vision. Such a meeting opens with a brief time of worship, after which the pastor proclaims the importance of cell-group ministry by motivating the troops and helping them get a handle on where they're headed.

Remember, each person present represents ministry to ten others. They are the VIPs of the church, the key to discipleship and growth.

What does the pastor need to say? "Go for it! Make it happen! Believe the Lord for great things!" Armed with exhortations from

Leadership Community
Three essential functions

Food for Champions

Chart 13

Scripture and inspiring illustrations, the pastor casts a vision that God will use to stimulate ministry.

I remember the time my pastor gave me, as one of his small-group leaders, a "Go get 'em boy" charge. Dr. Paul Cedar had recently come to the Lake Avenue Congregational Church, and he contacted a number of us parishioners with this request: "Some of our members have identified you as their small-group leader. Would you please meet with me next Sunday afternoon?"

At the meeting he said, "As your new pastor, I want you to know how important your ministry is. This congregation's too big for me to shepherd. You're the ones on the cutting edge, doing the real work." Predictably, we hung on his every word! He wasn't criticizing or taking over; he was affirming that our efforts were worthwhile.

"I'll do my best to cooperate and give you anything you need. We're in this together. I'm counting on you to handle the pastoring and believing that your people will thrive.

"I know you're studying various topics, but I'll work out my sermon outlines three weeks in advance and see to it that they're available to you, with Scripture references and discussion questions. If ever you need a lesson for your group, pick up an outline. If it's helpful, use it. If it's not helpful, don't worry. I want you to know I'm there for you, and I believe in what you're doing."

I went home and gave my wife, Grace, a rave review. "Pastor wants to help us. He'll provide sermon outlines and anything else we need. He said we could count on his backup."

Soon our pastor arranged a series of workshops for small-group leaders. He invited us to take the training we felt we needed. At each point of contact, he affirmed: "I'm counting on you to do the pastoring of the people in your group."

Then a sequence of phone calls began. One of the people in my small group rang us and gushed, "The adoption came through! I'm going to the hospital tomorrow to see our baby!"

I rejoiced with her.

The next day she called again. "Terrible news. The baby is irreparably, irreversibly brain damaged. We can't bring her home."

I tried to offer comfort.

Two hours later her husband called, worried about his wife's deep sorrow. My wife reassured him and counseled that he support her prayers.

Then the adoptive mother phoned me: "Come to the hospital, anoint our baby with oil, and pray for her so she'll be healed in Jesus' name."

My first thought was, *God, I don't want to do this.* I did not happen to be an elected church elder at that moment, and while the Bible does say that anyone sick can ". . . call the elders of the church . . ." to come, pray, and anoint (James 5:13–16) I reasoned it meant the current officers on staff. *Shouldn't the church staff go? I don't want to butt in between the senior minister and his flock.* At that moment, in my memory, I could hear the pastor say, "I'm counting on you to pastor these people." *If I phone the church office, he's likely to ask, "Have you gone yet?" or "Why not go and then call me?"* Because he had cast a vision. I knew I was the primary care person; the church staff was for backup, referral, and secondary care.[2] I was on point.

We drove to the hospital, anointed the baby with oil, and prayed for her, impressed with the deep faith of the mother. A miracle of God took place: The next week the family took her home healed and well, as confirmed by the pediatric neurologist. What joy and elation! Cell-group ministry was so stimulating I wanted to be even more involved. As I thanked God, I promised Him that the next time somebody described a brain injury, I'd offer to pray for it.

The next day I attended a dinner and sat near one of my prime business competitors. He mentioned that his daughter had long-standing brain damage. Again, my first thought was *God I don't want to do this!* The Lord brought to mind verses about keeping yesterday's vow. He didn't seem satisfied with my rationalization that it was a secret vow! *Don't you know that he's my business enemy? We sometimes feel strained when compared in public.* God seemed unpersuaded.

So I mumbled something to my competitor about what a shame his daughter's injury was and wondered if he would allow me to pray for her, very uneasy to be asking, but more uneasy to keep still.

His wife was present at the dinner and said, "Oh, wonderful. Come over to our house." Within a week or so, I drove to their house and prayed and am sad to report that the young woman didn't get well as the baby had.

A different kind of miracle occurred on the way to this man's home, however. I realized that I couldn't pray for his daughter while harboring any resentment and reservation. He wasn't an enemy; he belonged to the same spiritual team. We were merely business competitors! God provoked me to the point of repentance so I could love this girl and her family.

God was changing my life because of our cell-group involvement. Being a lay pastor with my wife had led me into spiritual ventures that we'd never have experienced otherwise. Working with a ten-person flock was exactly what God wanted us to do!

This kind of story helps achieve the purpose of the *V* function of a VHS meeting. It whets leaders' appetites and encourages them to seek out similar spiritual adventures. The process also allows the pastor the opportunity to affirm the rightness of shepherding a small group and of being the first line, and sometimes only line of pastoral care.

Vision casting places the locus of ministry where it belongs: in the hands of lay pastors. It commissions and stimulates these leaders. It reminds them that they have full permission to be mightily used of God. It shows how their responsibilities as leaders are firmly rooted in Scripture. It confirms that the ultimate call of Christ is to obedience, not merely to understanding. It makes them feel that others are praying for them, others can identify with them, and others are available for backup if needed.

The vision portion of the meeting presents a game plan with X's and Xa's in the center of the church's nurture and evangelism. Next comes the huddle.

Huddle. Typically, the huddle section centers around tables. Each L forms a cluster with his or her five X's, plus maybe an La or some Xa's who are learning the ropes. An observing D or Da may drop by and briefly perch on the periphery.

What happens? Under the L's direction and diagnostic coaching, the X's report their activities, celebrate their successes, and identify their problems. They plan; they propose solutions to difficulties; they hold each other accountable; they exhort one another; and they pray together (*see* Chart 14). This L–X team models the quality of caring desired in each X-led group.

Every X and Xa, as part of enlisting to be a cell-group leader, has pledged to place high priority on attendance at the VHS meeting and to complete a written report on the progress and needs of his or her cell. These reports assist many persons, from the senior leadership's planning to the computer database needed by the telecare groups (*see* Chapter 6). If any leader shows an unwillingness or lackadaisical attitude toward such accountability, the L or the D will soon counsel that person to pursue some other form of church ministry.

The L or La already knows about most of the cell-group and leadership circumstances, because he or she has been making on-site visits to the group. New X's need the L to drop by frequently, perhaps once a month. A more experienced X will profit from the L's coaching less frequently.

The L or La, along with the X or Xa, has also visited in the home of each cell-group member. They try to do this on an annual, if not semiannual, basis, in conjunction with a grand home visitation effort led by D's. Such personal, caring contacts with each household provide excellent background insights when situations arise that necessitate conflict resolution or difficult-member management.

While the L–X teams meet at one set of tables, the C's and Ca's— the leaders of groups of a hundred—meet with a D or Da at another (*see* Chart 15). Remember, the C's and L's don't account to each other. Instead, the D or Da coordinates the C meeting as the C's plan their next series of advertised activities. (D's meet with their L's by appointment outside the VHS meetings, as described in Chapter 11.)

The C's participation in the VHS keeps them tuned in to the vision of the church and guides them in how their groups can serve as fishing pools (or as Chapter 10 will describe it, as mezzanine units) for potential cell-group members.

These adult Bible-class teachers, departmental presidents, and the like, may occasionally bring their class officers or ministry teams to the VHS. Their attendance gives them direct access to the D or Da.

HUDDLES

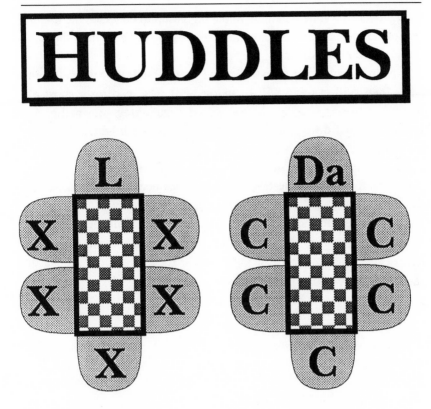

A time when coaches (L's, Da's) meet with lay ministers for

Report taking and celebrating
Problem identification & solving
Planning/anticipating/exhorting
sharing/praying

Chart 14

Skill. After everyone regathers into a big group to conclude the huddle section, perhaps with some testimonies for all to hear, then the skill portion of the VHS meeting begins.

If church health and growth depend on the quality of the cell ministry, then skill training will focus on what X's need to be most effective in their pastoring. I once asked a gathering of small-group leaders, "What do you need to know to do your job better?" I spent the next hour taking notes!

On another occasion, in a different part of the country, I asked a church staff a similar question: "What issues need to be addressed in the skill training of your X leaders?" The ideas they provided were almost identical to those on my first list. Here are their recommended topics for in-service and on-the-job training. Both evangelical and human-resource-development publishers offer a number of books on these how-to and small-group topics:

1. Listening.
2. Responding.
3. Challenging.
4. Confronting.
5. Evangelism.
6. Vision/strategy.
7. Leadership.
8. Recruitment.
9. Followup.
10. Nurturing.
11. Communicating the whole picture.
12. Administration.
13. Problem handling.
14. How to run a meeting.
15. How to facilitate sharing.
16. Counseling.
17. Discernment.
18. Credibility/example.
19. Spiritual knowledge.
20. Bible knowledge (lesson preparation).
21. How to reproduce apprentices (Xa's).
22. How to divide/birth a group.
23. How to make contacts with new prospects.
24. How to welcome newcomers.

25. Leading worship and music.
26. Identifying spiritual gifts.
27. How to link up with outreach projects.
28. When to ask for assistance.
29. How to pray for healing.
30. Managing disruptions.
31. Handling child care.
32. Deliverance.
33. Recognizing abuse.
34. Holistic health.
35. Time management.
36. Loyalty/teamwork.
37. Affirmation.
38. Attitudes.
39. Conflict management.
40. Personal disciplines.
41. How to teach about prayer.
42. How to listen to God in prayer.
43. Referrals.
44. Legal implications.
45. Confidentiality.
46. How to share ministry as a team.
47. Overcoming shyness.
48. Stewardship/budgeting.
49. Pastor/shepherd skills.
50. One-on-one discipling skills.

A word of caution: No one can impose skill training on existing group leaders. Such attempts will draw resentment. Someone can, however, assemble existing X's and L's and ask, "Could you help me create a curriculum that will give you the skill training you desire to be better lay pastors?"

If they brainstorm and develop their own list, which will probably be quite similar to the topics itemized above, then the pastor can ask them if they'd be willing to invest some time in studying these issues.

In one situation, I, as a visiting consultant, raised that question to a group of Bible-study leaders. The pastoral staff had already warned me, "These people refuse to participate in training programs." After helping me assemble a list of helpful topics, the participants turned the query back to me: "How much time will it take you to help us learn all these topics?'' I suggested one night every two weeks for the next ten months. "We'll do it!" they said.

Why such a positive response? I had addressed their felt needs and treated them as adult learners. I wasn't imposing solutions to problems they hadn't recognized; I helped them identify and organize their problems and responded to their request for aid.

Most pastors desire to train their people. They also have access to excellent curriculum resources. In fact, one of the responsibilities of the D is to approve the teaching themes and curriculum that will be made available to the group leaders. What most ministers lack is the grand game plan: a churchwide design for commissioning lay pastors with a vision for spiritual ministry and then equipping them with the skills they need to make disciples effectively. (*See* Chart 16.)

How Can X's and Xa's Best Work Together?

The Jethro II model and the VHS leadership community functions both pursue the same goal: ensuring healthy cell groups. They also utilize the same methodology: focusing on cell-group leadership.

In particular, the Meta-Church system creates a climate for leadership development based on the model of assigning an X or Xa a responsibility and *then* offering on-the-job supervision and ongoing training (OJT). The sequence is: assign, supervise, train.

By contrast, the familiar academic pattern adopted by most churches is for someone to graduate from training and then get a job, usually with little effective supervision. In other words: train, assign, and perhaps supervise.

This age-old approach doesn't work well because adults tend to focus only on what's immediately in their foreview. The world of human distress is too big for general study; cell leaders must have a specific assignment if they are to be motivated to learn. VHS training and one-on-one L–X supervision concentrate on the teachable moments when adult leaders are engaging in actual ministry. After all, everyone becomes motivated to learn how to handle a situation when the alternative is to fall face forward!

Leadership community meetings take place with every-other-week frequency for a practical reason: morale is critical! Most cutting-edge leaders can't wait much longer for group encouragement! Leaders who miss a meeting due to illness or travel have to carry their burdens and questions for a whole month before they can be prayed over in their next L–X group.

The X and Xa need the shared experience of receiving such training as a team. Veteran cell-group leaders, however, won't be stimulated by certain basic training designed for new Xa's. The D or Da will therefore occasionally pull the apprentice leaders into a separate class of first-year skill curriculum. The net result should reinforce the X–Xa relationship; the D will tell the Xa the same kinds of things that the X has been saying and modeling.

How do these X's and Xa's work together in forming a new cell group? Field observations have helped identify at least three widespread birthing protocols. (*See* Chart 17.)

"Birth Type A" occurs when an apprentice leader, rising through a cell, is commissioned off into a new cell. The first job of this prospective X is to find a new Xa, since no new cell can begin without both an X and an Xa (and an H). This future X may have to look no further than the fellow members of the mother cell. Or, he or she may receive "fishing pool" help from the D's, C's, and L's. Some churches, such as New Hope Community Church mentioned in Chapter 6, host a biannual Super Bowl Weekend to highlight opportunities for service in cell ministry.

Chart 17 identifies the rising Xa through a notation system of double parentheses and single parentheses; the progrssion starts with "someone out there" (double parentheses), who moves to rising Xa status (single parentheses), and who, ultimately, becomes a bona fide Xa (no parentheses).

"Birth Type B" happens when the cell leader says to the apprentice, "You're strong enough now to lead this group. I'm heading out to form a new cell." This exiting X will likewise need to secure a new Xa and H before the new cell can be officially organized.

"Birth Type C" takes place when both the X and the Xa are new. This kind of cell is often catalyzed through a Super Bowl Weekend or other high-visibility event. Such a strong, centralized program conveys this vision to newcomers and marginally involved people: "We'd like to give you a 'license' to recruit your own cell and be part of an exciting opportunity for nurture and leadership development." The notation system in this case begins with a seeker who hasn't even been recruited into the cell (an "S" in double parentheses), who becomes a growing Christian and, eventually, an apprentice cell leader (an Xa) and then a cell leader (an X).

Jethro II

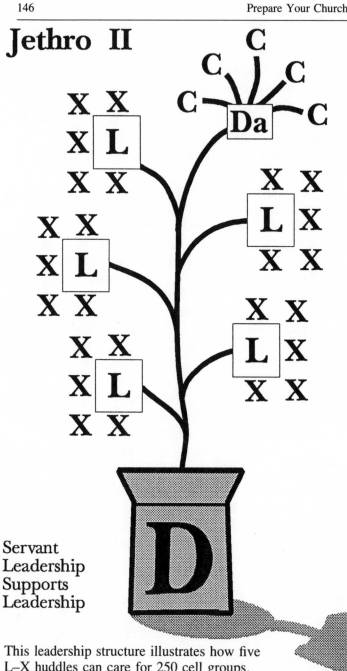

**Servant
Leadership
Supports
Leadership**

This leadership structure illustrates how five
L–X huddles can care for 250 cell groups.
By adding up to five more L–X huddles, a staff
pastor (D) can carry 50 cells or 500 participants.

Chart 15

X and Xa Development

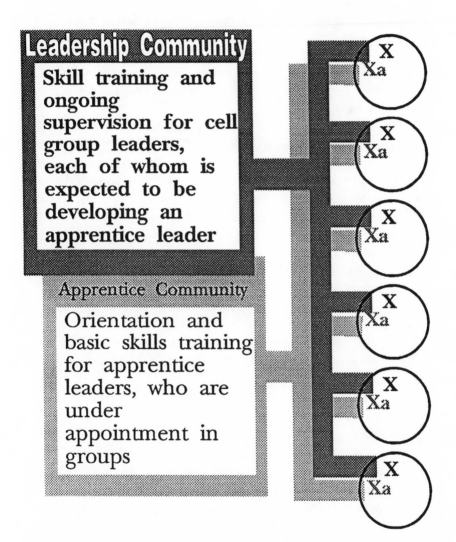

Chart 16

Birth types "A" and "B" are the inevitable results when a cell group grasps the vision for reproducing itself. Our early indicators suggest that about two-thirds of cells will be able to find apprentices from within themselves. Another third of the apprentice leaders will probably need to be recruited centrally and placed in sponsoring cells to replace apprentices who spin off, move out of town, or drop away for other reasons.

Most X's, therefore, start off in the Xa role. If their track record commends their skills as someone able to birth a group (seniority and prestige carry very little weight), the Xa receives an appointment from the L to become an X.

Most X's choose not to become L's, especially if their gift mix lacks diagnostic skills and training abilities, and they do not have the time required to be an effective L. Instead, they become, in due time, "senior X's" who grow new X's and repeatedly go through the mitosis. The Meta-Church honors those persons who facilitate mutual ministry. Therefore the creation and encouragement of the X role is the critical event for church growth.

Whatever avenue God uses to cultivate and recruit the new Xa, cell leaders maintain their role by birthing new groups. The health of their cells therefore depends on a solid partnership with their Xa's—an objective that every part of the church organization seeks to spur: The people of the small group want to be shepherded by harmonious leadership; the L's coach their charges on sound X-Xa relationships; and the D's facilitate the skills that affirm the importance of a cell group's leaders.

Can cell group health be guaranteed? No. But this attention to caring for leaders who, in turn, care for their people will prepare the structures which, when prayerfully operated, will activate effective one-another ministry.

One day soon, North American churches of twenty-five to fifty thousand will appear in every major metropolitan area. In them, district pastors (D's) will spend most of their time in visitation, in order to nurture and disciple their coaches (L's) and their leaders of congregation-size groups (C's).

The pivotal roles in the church will be those of the cell-group leader (X) and the apprentice leader (Xa). The entire church structure will be organized to equip these men and women to shepherd and reproduce their flocks of ten.

The results? The worldwide harvest field of over 5 billion souls will be evangelized and discipled as never before.

Cell Birthing Protocols

Typical Group Maturity at Time of Birth = 24 Meetings

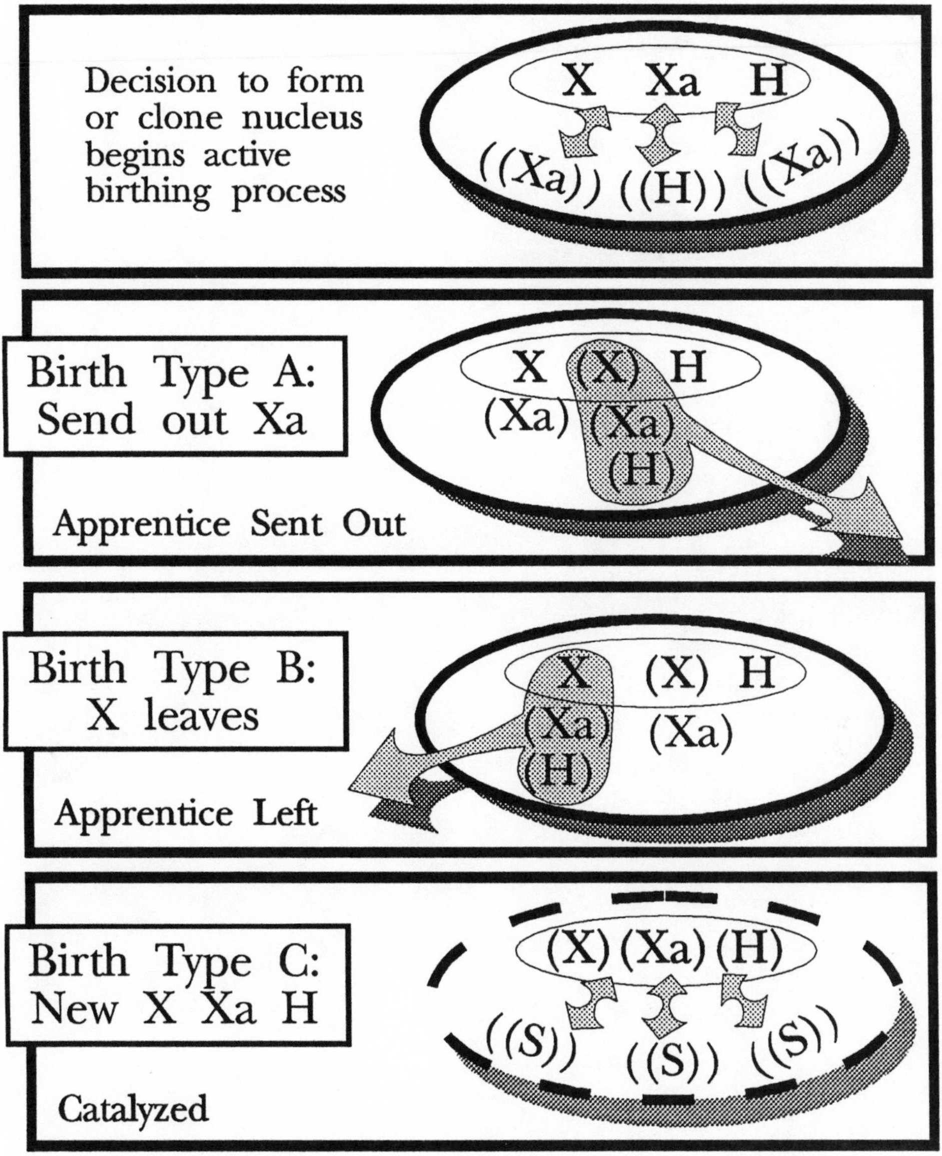

Decision to form
or clone nucleus
begins active
birthing process

X Xa H

$((Xa))$ $((H))$ $((Xa))$

Birth Type A:
Send out Xa

X (X) H
(Xa) (Xa)
(H)

Apprentice Sent Out

Birth Type B:
X leaves

X (X) H
(Xa) (Xa)
(H)

Apprentice Left

Birth Type C:
New X Xa H

(X) (Xa) (H)

$((S))$ $((S))$ $((S))$

Catalyzed

Chart 17

SECTION IV

What to Visualize for the Big Picture

10
Think Panoramically With the Metaglobe

As a consultant who deals with churches across several-dozen denominations, I rarely encounter laziness or insincerity. Most church leaders, both lay and professional, are highly motivated, faithful, gifted, hard-working people.

Why, then, has their problem not yielded to their efforts? Frequently I find that they've misread the difficulty. They're putting their whole hearts into ministry, but are giving attention to the wrong trees in the forest of possible concerns.

How can they solve that dilemma? I try to walk these leaders from the base of one tree to the top of the hill above the forest. They've lost their objectivity about what's happening or what should occur in the forest as a whole. They need help in maintaining perspective. I guide them to redefine their quandary in terms they can understand and then to assess where they're going and what they're trying to do.

As my staff and I trained our clients to develop their own interpretive skills, we created an easily understood diagnostic system. It enables leaders to back off and see the whole as well as how one part of their ministry affects other parts.

We call the tool we use the "metaglobe." The bulk of this chapter will explain how we map out a metaglobe and use it to maintain perspective on growth, application of energies, extent of problems, and interconnecting between one effect and another.

Paths to the Future

First, however, let me summarize the underlying assumptions on which the Meta-Church capitalizes:

1. Churches of the future will be committed to making more and better disciples. Anything less won't do. The mark of discipleship goes beyond a decision of salvation, a pleasant experience of fellowship, or an identity of providing cold water in Jesus' name. It calls men, women, girls, and boys to confess the Lord Jesus as Savior. It summons them to identify themselves in one-another ministry through responsible involvement with a local church.

Disciple-making churches, in turn, need certain tools, such as a viable system of quality small groups, that can encourage this kind of obedience.

2. Churches of the future will be more concerned with the size of the harvest than with the capacity of their facilities. They're keenly aware that God established His plan of redemption without tabulating the seating capacity of their church building, even if filled two or three times over! They envision a huge, unreached harvest of human souls for whom Christ died. God wants to empower them, they believe, for a scope of ministry far greater than even their most recent building committee has imagined.

Therefore, as they plan, they abandon the notions of containment implied in such questions as, "How much pew space remains until we're full?" and "What's the maximum crowd our parking lot or classroom space can accommodate?" They know that the Meta-Church model of cell multiplication allows for virtually unlimited growth and that multiple services and even multiple campuses may be required to service it.

3. Churches will be known primarily as caring places rather than as teaching associations. These churches of the future realize that God measures His people more by their obedience than by their knowledge of Bible facts. Therefore, they've shifted their priorities from teaching to caring, from understanding to application.

They concede that many churches' lack of attendance stems from the truth contained in a widespread stereotype: Churches are uncaring places with a lot of rules that haven't been made relevant to people's lives. The remedy to this dilemma, they are convinced, involves engaging people with the Christ of the Bible and His teachings in the context of a nurturing small group.

4. Pastors will genuinely encourage ministry by the laity, despite centuries of modeling to the contrary. They've shaken off the image of clergy as hired hands whose job is to do the ministry for the church. They've demonstrated to the parishioners that they're not merely paying lip service to an in-vogue idea or limiting lay ministry to a smattering of children's programs and adult custodial duties. These clergy of the future have removed the OFF LIMITS signs from every level of pastoral care. They've restructured the training and organization of the entire church to enable every willing person to find a quality opportunity for life-changing ministry.

5. Lay-ministry assignments will involve leadership of a group. In churches of the future, a significant percentage of the people will each take responsibility for the spiritual well-being of a set of others who meet regularly as a group of ten or so. These trained and supervised lay shepherds will not perpetrate shallow, arm's-length blessings and prayers. Rather, through a context of relationships, they offer ongoing intensive care to real life's war zone of the walking wounded. They affirm that people can improve relational skills, rebuild shattered dreams, achieve freedom from negative attitudes and destructive habits, and learn to give support to one another.

6. Laity, given the opportunity, will invest time, energy, and money to learn the skills required to do a competent job of pastoring. Based on the competent and effective modeling of their senior pastor or pastoral staff, they take ministry to a limited-size group so seriously that they choose it over elected office or honorific titles. Most growing Christians prefer disciple making to policy making, hands-on ministry to hands-tied committees, and challenging people situations to safe administrative isolation.

7. Finally, in the church of the future, pastors and people will remain dependent on the Holy Spirit to make His gifts available for mutually edifying one-another ministry. They acknowledge that if the Holy Spirit were to cease His workings, no handbook or set of principles could replace the guidance, conviction, and enthusiasm traceable to His infilling. The Meta-Church model of ministry can remain operative only if the Holy Spirit isn't grieved, quenched, or otherwise prevented from effectively ministering.

Introducing the Metaglobe

These seven assumptions jolt the thinking patterns of most Western-trained Christians, both clergy and laity. As a result, we require help in mentally mapping out the Meta-Church. We also need a new vocabulary for discussing the Meta-Church and adapting the circumstances of each particular congregation to it.

The *metaglobe* does just that. It uses the familiar three-dimensional sphere found in many classrooms and homes to provide a number of analogies for the social architecture of the church of the future. Here's how it works:

> Entire globe = entire Meta-Church
> Continents = large-group meetings
> Islands = small-group meetings
> Axis = coordination linkage
> International date line = focus on how newcomers feel
> Atmosphere = prayer
> Oceans = populations, both members and nonmembers in the
> church's primary service area, who are not present in one of the
> meetings

At this point we must discard a few aspects of the globe of Planet Earth. The Meta-Church has no temperature range; each section of this world is just as delightful as another. And it lacks political association; so the northern (or upper) hemisphere holds no superiority over the southern (or lower) hemisphere.

In fact, every healthy believer will be charted at least twice and will be found in both hemispheres—once in a cell group (which has arbitrarily been placed in a certain portion of the southern hemisphere) and once in corporate worship (a section of the northern hemisphere). (*See* Chart 18.) In general the large events are mapped onto the northern hemisphere and the smaller events on the southern hemisphere.

A final change involves the coloring of the globe. Let's replace the typical blue oceans, white polar caps, tan deserts, and so on, with the following colors, using the parenthetical memory aids:

> *Purple* (think purple robes of ceremonial pomp) for governance.
>
> *Gray* (or silver, as in quarters, nickels, and dimes) for finances.
>
> *Red* (fire engines in a parade) for worship celebration.
>
> *Orange* ("construction" traffic signs) for extension and auxiliary.
>
> *Yellow* (Yellow Brick Road) for bridging and mezzanine.
>
> *Green* (peas in a pod) for nurture groups and ministry teams.
>
> *Blue* (lettering on an ambulance) for telecare and counseling.

This order (*see* Chart 19) follows the color patterns of a painter's pallet. Except for the gray, which has a special role, the regions blend into one another, which will remind us later that we can glide around the globe in creating intentional migration patterns.

The schema, by the way, bears no relevance to the symbols and patterns used in certain New Age artistry. God, author of the universe, created all colors and affirmed that they may be used to His glory, such as in the Tabernacle's design and in its priests' clothing (Exodus 26, 28). Heaven likewise will dazzle with gorgeous color (Revelation 4:2, 3; 21:9–21)—why not our conception of the church as well?

Here's how the metaglobe looks so far.

All areas on the metaglobe represent meetings, with two exceptions. First, the atmosphere (analogous to the unseen spiritual realm and prayer) is the life breath of all that happens. If polluted or nonexistent, nothing will last. Thus the atmosphere is everywhere.

Second, finances (gray) play a role in every ministry, so we can add some gray outlines to any color as needed.

Let's look at each zone in greater detail, and then we'll put the map to work:

Purple Zone. The *governance* of a church involves the councils, boards, committees, and church staff itself. This zone links with other

Simplified
Metaglobe

Axis

Large Group
Celebration

Small Groups

Atmosphere

Chart 18

META-ZONES

N.C.D. = New Church Development
C.R.T. = Crisis Response Teams
M.O.D. = Minister of the Day

Chart 19

zones by way of the axis. After describing all the zones, I'll suggest some specific committees that could be on the axis.

Gray Region. *Finances* affect every aspect of the church, but primarily the purple zone. Leaders who influence the church must deal soundly with its budgets and business side if their people work is to endure.

Red Zone. Church *celebration* activities, for the most part, require the use of the sanctuary. A red-zone event is something big and festive, held in the main worship room.

"Continents" in the red zone, proportionally sized, represent the scheduled worship service. A church with two services, for instance, will sketch a small continent for the lesser-attended early service and a large one for the packed-out eleven o'clock gathering. Additional "continents" can depict special Christmas, Easter, or other large plenary events.

Because red-zone events are complex productions, we need to insert some small squares in them. These are task forces associated with large meetings. The following chart places such crowd facilitation task forces as ushers, translators, and nursery workers in the lower portion of the red zone. Musical teams, drama groups and other up-front leadership groups go in the upper portion. (*See* Chart 20.)

Orange Zone. According to the artist's pallet, orange comes between red and yellow. Since this zone serves as a *catchall*, under-construction category *for extension and auxiliary* ministries, it will receive attention after all the other zones have been covered.

Yellow Zone. Changing hemispheres, we reach the *mezzanine or bridge zone*. It often contains congregation-size seminar-type meetings of between 25 and 175 people. These attractive events, orchestrated by C's (leaders of a hundred) draw church people from other color zones as well as outsiders. As a result, yellow-zone events, if properly planned, can serve as "fishing pools" for new contacts, such as potential cell-group members.

Bridging occurs whenever outsiders find relevance in what is happening in ongoing meetings like a large Sunday school's adult Bible fellowship or in occasional events like a three-day family-life confer-

Mapping Larger Meetings in the Red Zone

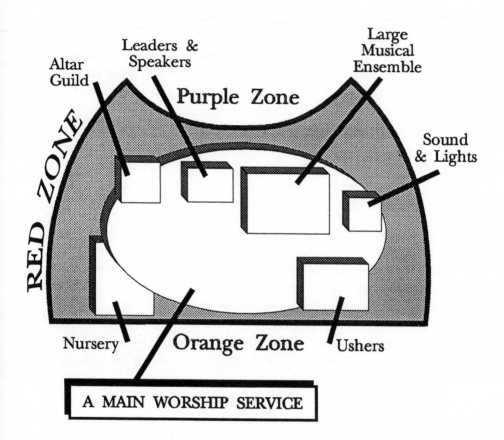

Chart 20

ence or group golf lessons offered by a church member who is the neighborhood pro.

The Acquaintance Making Place (AMP) function of a yellow zone activity shows up on the metaglobe as a plus sign ($+$), representing four chairs toe to toe for round-robin interaction. For example, the above-mentioned golf foursomes provide an excellent forum for churched and unchurched people to establish a conversational rapport. So does the meet-your-neighbor mixer at the conclusion of each session at the family-life conference. (*See* Chart 21.)

In C-led groups, people need a minimum of three or four minutes per person for acquaintance-making activities, such as answering Serendipity questions in foursomes. This means a foursome would require twelve–sixteen minutes on the agenda. If these foursomes include an X or Xa, the other individuals have an ideal forum for being exposed to the personality of a cell-group leader or apprentice leader.

Green Zone. The *cell or small-group zone* contains nurture groups and certain categories of ministry teams. A green-zone event is any small group meeting in a home, or even on premises, in which people receive nurture and intimate encouragement.

The green-zone groups are assembled by X group leaders and are affinity-based ministry to individuals (X–I cells), Evangelism is practiced within these small groups. They are supported by the VHS leadership training system with its L–X and D–C groups. Groups from other colors, such as support or recovery group leaders from the blue zone, come to the green zone for VHS training and return to the blue zone for ministry in twelve-step groups.

Each nurture group in the green zone is diagrammed by a small circle. Squares, as in the red zone, represent task groups. The more nurturing that takes place, the more circular the shapes.

The VHS meetings can build on this color schema to remind everyone of how all ministries contribute to the whole. Each huddle table could have a plaid tablecloth. Red plaid goes on the group handling the ushering, outside parking, and altar counseling. Green goes to nurture groups and task groups like those who take food to the poor. Blue goes on the table with the telecare shift leaders and the twelve-step group leaders for recovering alcoholics. And yellow goes on the table of C's.

Blue Zone. Located at the southernmost part of the metaglobe, the

Yellow Zone: Making Use of Medium-size Groups for Bridging and Mezzanine

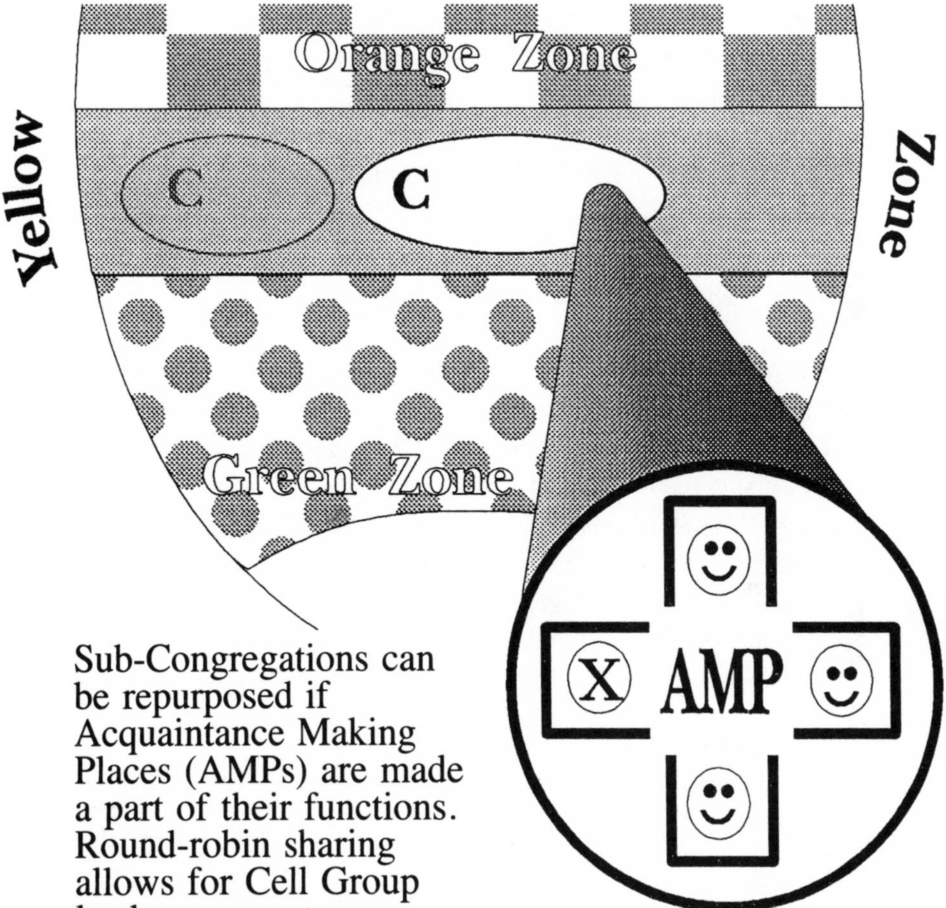

Sub-Congregations can be repurposed if Acquaintance Making Places (AMPs) are made a part of their functions. Round-robin sharing allows for Cell Group leaders to meet new people.

Chart 21

blue zone includes telecare, psychologically intensive ministries, and traditional pastoral care. Here is where those are reached out to who won't join or aren't currently part of a group. Any church circumstances that require the attention of a professional clinician, an ordained clergyperson, or a specially trained care person are also based in the blue zone.

Blue-zone activities therefore range from psychologically supported treatment of dysfunctional people to classic pastoral visitation of shut-ins and the bereaved. The blue zone covers support groups, therapy groups, pastoral counseling, lay helpers in clinical counseling of EGRs, telecare team telephoning, deacon ministry, Stephen Ministry, walk-in needs, governmental social service requests, funerals, and weddings. (Chapter 6 described support, therapy, and telecare groups. Chapters 7 and 8 presented EGRs. Chapters 6 and 8 analyzed deacon ministries.)

Prayer ministries outside the major worship services can also be labeled as blue zone.

As in the other zones, small circles represent nurture groups and small squares task groups. (*See* Chart 22.)

None of the metaglobe color zones is exclusive. People, for example, can be part of a green-zone primary care circle while visiting a blue-zone circle for auxiliary care. Or some may be attracted to the church through a yellow-zone bridge event, such as a workshop on divorce recovery, where they take part in an acquaintance exercise (mixer). The church then walks these people down into the blue zone for followup. After a while they'll be ready for green-zone nurture groups.

People in groups tend to have fewer unmet needs than those who don't participate in nurturing relationships. Nevertheless, the telephone safety net in the blue zone regularly tries to poll *all* the households of the church. This form of secondary care is a necessary redundancy in an effective church system. Telecare is not an optional ministry in the church of the future.

The information received by the telecare teams can trigger the dispatch of their backup group, an emergency squad, perhaps of deacons, or of Stephen Ministries, called a crisis response team (CRT). Or the telecare staff might extend an invitation to a relevant support group.

Meta-Map

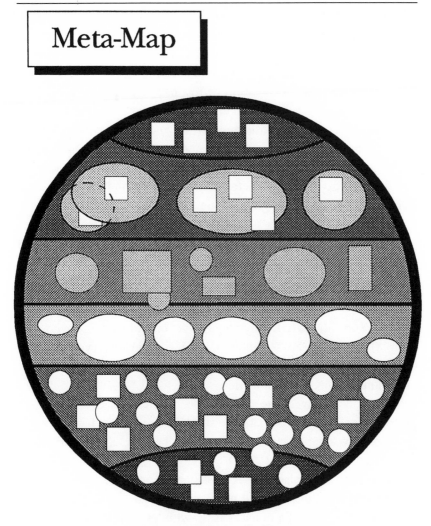

Mapping of Groups Which Meet One or More Times per Month

Chart 22

People with certain crucial needs can't wait for the normal mass-marketing advertising system to get word to them.

Blue-zone support group leaders (X's) receive their coaching from clinically trained or clinically coached supervisors (L's), such as the licensed psychologist who would be retained to teach telecare people how to conduct interventions in crisis situations.

These psychological consultants are not merely once-a-week, one-on-one counselors; they are administrators or trainers for a small-group system. They transfer their skills to the small-group leaders so as to develop an increasingly competent ministry team. And they advise cell leaders on referrals and legal liabilities, serving as expert witnesses in court if need be! In today's litigious environment, all counseling beyond peer-level suggestions must be sensitive to the question, "What will this sound like in front of a jury?"

Staff people (D's) with a penchant for psychological training skills are likewise assigned to the blue zone.

Orange Zone Revisited. Anything not yet categorized as governance (purple), finance (gray), celebration (red), congregation (yellow), nurture cell (green), or backup pastoral care (blue) falls into the arena of extension and auxiliary ministries.

Life in the orange zone can include businesslike cost centers or related organizations, such as radio stations, bookstores, tape libraries, Christian day schools, child-care facilities, health clubs, or retirement homes.

The orange zone also houses missionary concerns, from overseas missions to cross-cultural home missions, from youth-group projects in the Dominican Republic to partnership with local para-church organizations. Political action and other we-care-about-our-community undertakings are likewise orange zone.

Within bigger churches, denominational relationships base themselves in the orange zone. In smaller churches and where the denomination is closely connectional, denominational affairs will usually go in the purple zone.

Certain educational functions are orange zone. Academic-style adult Christian-education institutes usually stay in the orange zone. So do classes like the Bethel Bible series, which deepen people's spiritual lives and offer systematic teaching. Although they function as legitimate ministries, unless they directly contribute to processing people into the cells, they're classified as auxiliary.

Children's Sunday School? The classic pre-K through grade twelve Sunday-school program fits in one of three places. If it takes place in large groups, simultaneously with the worship service, it can be mapped as a shade-on organization near its adult counterpart meeting in the red zone. If it meets before or after the worship, it's spread between the yellow (departmental assembly) and green (classes). If the church leadership is reevaluating the role of Sunday school, it may be parked temporarily in the orange zone. An orange-zone placement might signal that Sunday school has lost its drawing power or that its classes are not effectively open to newcomers.

What does the future look like in terms of the spiritual formation of children? First, as I pointed out in Chapter 8, those churches with effective Sunday schools will make only minor adjustments, as long as their system works.

Others will experiment with off-premises neighborhood meetings, combining ideas like Boy and Girl Scouts with Child Evangelism Fellowship's backyard Bible clubs (green zone). When the children do come to church on Sunday, they might, as one big group, watch a Christian version of "Sesame Street," performed by crack teams of talented artists (shadow events in the red zone). Occasional retreats to which guests are invited might look like Scouting Jamborees, so could be considered in the yellow zone.

I'm not proposing that anyone completely do away with Sunday school. And I can't point to cases where the cell system has fully replaced children's Sunday school. Rather, I suggest repurposing and reorganizing by asking significant questions. For example: What opportunities are being missed by holding AWANA, Christian Service Brigade, and Pioneer Clubs on premises instead of in the neighborhoods? We studied one situation and found that up to seven times as many children could be reached, per dollar, off premises as on!

Or what about curriculum? Surely a church's divine calling goes beyond the feeding of their denomination's publishing house.

If a curriculum does not feed the felt needs of the students, do not prefer it simply because it encourages a denominational tie. An elaborate Sunday-school curriculum may prove less successful than a sim-

ple sheet of instructions that direct more personal Bible study.
Remember, publishing organizations may be so committed to perpet-
uating their own existence that they miss the mark when it comes to the
needs of the class.

Whatever new tools come our way, the Christian home must become
a more effective agent of religious education for children. Scripture
describes the Jewish family as the locus of spiritual formation (Deuteronomy 6:4–9). Since cell groups do a better job than any other
method we know of helping Dad and/or Mom learn to converse about
Christ, then the church, through its cell ministry, will be supporting the
household as the primary religious education organization in society.

Purple Zone (AXIS) Revisited. Chart 23 shows the center spine or
axis of the metaglobe. It details how all church staff activities are
arranged to support various surface activities. Five nontraditional staff
committees, particularly apt for coordinating and administering, are
shown on that chart: a Guilds, Troupes, and Forums Committee (purple to red), a financial performance review (purple/gray to orange's
bookstores and schools), a meeting, calendar, interpretation, and facilitation center (purple to yellow's need to coordinate marketing), a
VHS coordinating committee (purple to green), and a pastoral care and
psychology coordination group (purple to blue).

Taking the Metaglobe for a Spin

Now the fun begins! The purpose of the metaglobe is to represent the
meetings of a church and define whether they occur at the cell level
(green and blue zones), the mid-size-group level (yellow zone), or the
very large group level (red zone). These colors parallel the cell, congregation, and celebration dynamics described in Chapters 4 and 5.

A goal of the Meta-Church is to multiply large numbers of green-
zone groups so that people can be nurtured and loved toward maturity
in Christ. Thus leaders, with relative ease, can use the metaglobe to
observe and discuss the strengths and needs of their fellowship.

Planning teams of staff and lay leaders who attend Fuller Evangelistic Association Meta-Church Cluster Consultations learn to shove
activities across borders, manipulate the colors, and do whatever else
is helpful to visualize: How could this ministry better represent what
God wants our church to accomplish?

META-AXIS

Policy, Personnel,
Nominations, Long
Range Planning

Finance, Missions, Buildings
Capital Gifts, Administration

Marketing, Calendar, Venue,
Interpretation (Promotion)

Counseling,
TeleCare,
Intake

Chart 23

Ask deep questions like: Why is such-and-such group on the globe? What does it contribute to the whole? What does it need from the whole? How does it connect? The technical term for these understandings is a group's *System Interface Function* (SIF).

Proportioning the Zones

As presented in Chapter 4, healthy churches must have at least two sizes of groups: large celebration (red zone) and small cell (green zone). Although the cells are the engine that propels the church forward, small groups will seem to lack significance if they're not joined to (or alternated with) a praise celebration of corporate worship. Cells support the celebration, and the celebration gives significance to the cell strategy. Therefore red and green zones are essential. So is some degree of purple-zone senior leadership to coordinate it all.

How much blue zone should a church have? As much telecare and other group ministry as is necessary to minister to two kinds of people: those who haven't joined a group and EGRs who would otherwise cripple a green-zone group. In other words, a church needs as many blue groups as are necessary to keep the green groups spiritually fit.

What about orange zone? Many of these extension and auxiliary programs need to be repurposed or broadened so that they support the cell ministries. For example, Lutheran churches often sponsor private day schools, open to any family in their vicinity. The parent-teacher fellowships are usually a highly fertile pond for "fishing" for the unchurched.

The pastor could say to the principal, "Let's include some of our X's to fellowship with this parent group. Help us create a mixer in your program that affords opportunities for social acquaintance making." This approach does not leave group finding to chance. Plus, such an assimilation strategy would be far more successful than the more common method of inviting the parents to a Lutheran worship service. The liturgical culture shock may be more than the school family is prepared to endure.

How about yellow zone? As with the orange, church strategists can create intentional migration patterns whose ultimate destination is the green zone.

For example, remember the golf foursomes noted earlier in this chapter as "plusses" in the yellow zone? Those icons for foursomes will be colored green. The implication is that new prospects will be referred to cells in the green zone. Or some of the yellow-zone plusses from the family-life seminar could be coded blue. This color would indicate that attenders will be encouraged to join a blue-zone support and recovery group until they're ready to be part of a green-zone nurture cell.

Or upon reflecting about a certain congregation-size group, a pastor may conclude: "This yellow group has no acquaintance-making place (AMP) plus mark. That means that people may not be moving beyond the drinking-coffee-together stage. We need to add an AMP component. This change will help the small-group leaders who attend meet new people by taking part in a round-robin get-acquainted time."

Any discussion about these AMP plus-sign mixers will begin to probe the deeper issue of Affinity Facilitation Structures (AFS). Much has been written, especially by Lyman Coleman, on how to get people to open up by using skillfully crafted self-disclosure questions. It takes skill to help people get to know each other.

What About Visitors?

Once church leaders have mapped all the group meetings, they can review the migrations of visitors. The international date line serves as a prompt to ask in every color zone: Are we handling things as we should with regard to newcomers?

For example, a front-door church (*see* Chapter 5), will pay special attention to the date line as it passes through the red zone. Does the church have a clear strategy for moving these guests from the red zone to the yellow to the green? Does it have enough greeters and registration methods in each plenary meeting to see that newcomer information is captured? Does it do tours of the building, offer a five-minute slide show, or take guests around a briefing room filled with photo exhibits? (*See* Chart 24.)

Or if the yellow-zone congregation-sized groups attract lots of members' acquaintances, think about the date line as it passes through the yellow zone. Ascertain the status of a pastor's, seeker's, or new member's class. Evaluate whether newcomers receive an invitation to the

META-ZONES

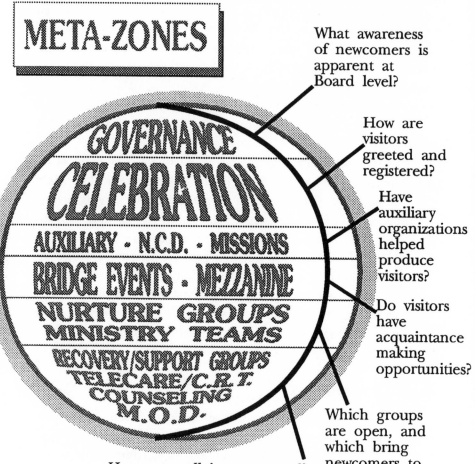

What awareness of newcomers is apparent at Board level?

How are visitors greeted and registered?

Have auxiliary organizations helped produce visitors?

Do visitors have acquaintance making opportunities?

Which groups are open, and which bring newcomers to events?

How are walk-ins processed? Are newcomers phoned? Do counselees receive invitations?

International Date Line

Adds Newcomer and New Member Observations

Chart 24

pastor's home or to the house of some other highly visible member.

Formulate appropriate questions for the green zone: Are the cell groups open? Are they functioning as initial entry points for side-door recruits?

Now check the yellow zone for green plusses. Without them, newcomers won't move toward the better pastoral care of the green zone.

For example, suppose one of the yellow groups is a four-week new member's class run by the pastor. If it lasts an hour, could the presentation be limited to forty-five minutes? In the remaining fifteen minutes, newcomers can be directed and assisted to make acquaintances. If X's and Xa's are invited, and if they've been coached by their L's in how to behave, each new member will have a positive interaction with four leaders, one each week. Each X and Xa, in turn, will have met twelve people they can now call by name. The likelihood of finding affinity—and thus potential cell membership—is quite good.

Yellow-zone events can go even further in feeding new contacts to the cells. The C's who arranged the agenda can ask recent guests, "Of the group leaders you've met, with whom could you relate best in a small group setting? If you'll rank them one, two, three, on a piece of paper, we'll arrange a further meeting." The C's pass these qualified leads on to the X's and Xa's. This approach is far superior to the idea of an X standing around the coffee pot, hoping that the coffee is so hot that he or she can make one new contact before everyone's brew cools enough to drink up.

How does a church attract new blood to the yellow-zone meeting? C's have a whole world of possible choices. One of the most helpful marketing approaches involves dividing the general population into age or stage-of-life divisions. Then the C's target one of those categories. Here are some examples:

Age-Life Stage Divisions

Teens—jr. high
Teens—sr. high
College
Young singles—early career
Divorced persons
Single parent—with new baby

Single parent—with elementary-age child(ren)
Single parent—with teen(s)
Single parent—empty nest
Young married—pregnant
Young married—with new baby
Married—with elementary-age child(ren)
Married—with teen(s)
Married—early empty nest
Married—empty nest
Widowed
Retirees
Self-employed
Jet-set employment
Unemployed
Seasonal visitors, vacationers, tourists, snowbirds
Women—not on career track
Women—career

Suppose the pastor gives the C an assignment: "Take the young marrieds and come up with something special and appealing to them." What are the options?

The C begins inquiring about felt needs. Again, the possibilities are endless:

Program Designs and Interpretation
Example: Young Married—Early Nester Stage

Answering children's questions about God, heaven, death
Baby-sitting and daycare
Budget and finance
Career development
Communication skills
Conflict management
Entertainment
Goal setting
In-laws
Marriage enrichment
Parenting
Sexual adjustment

Social interaction with peers
Stress management
Toilet training
Two-career households
Values transmission

The C finds a credible speaker or compelling topic, creates the event, advertises it in places the young marrieds will notice, invites X's and Xa's, and *voila!* The C has created a strategy of reaching out to an age-stage division that can start a migration pattern downward into the green zone.

Another approach feeds prospects from the blue zone's telecare teams, support groups, and others upward to the green. (*See* Chart 25.)

Why Age-Life Stage Over Geography?

I've introduced the pioneering work of Paul Yonggi Cho in several previous chapters. He divided Seoul, Korea, into geographic areas, like postal zones, and assigned staff accordingly. This approach made a lot of sense in light of the semiannual grand home visitation blitz in which Dr. Cho's staff visits every household in the church.

North American Meta-Churches, such as New Hope Community Church in Portland, Oregon (introduced in Chapter 6 and profiled in Chapter 12), find that "specialty districts"—for women, young marrieds, the developmentally disabled, and so on—are relatively easy to program. This structure based on felt needs is what I term the age-life stage divisions.

I recommend that most churches start with age-life stage divisions. They're relatively easy to target and to organize. The affinity dynamics, as stressed in the deacon section of Chapter 8, work better with age-life stage than geography. Program portfolios readily evolve for teens, collegians, young singles, mature singles, couples in the nesting stage, career women, homemaking women, senior citizens, and so on.

These yellow-zone-based divisions, led by D's and C's, can develop their own networks of green- and blue-zone events coached by L's and shepherded by X's. Conventional churches can begin transitioning toward Meta-Church models by emphasizing cell groups and VHS training within the structure of each age-life stage division.

As the cell ministry broadens and spreads over a huge square mile-

Meta-Map

Moving from Blue activities up into Green

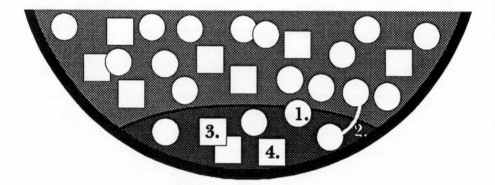

1. Some whole groups graduate as their recovery progresses.
2. Individuals graduate and find growth groups as their recovery progresses.
3. Telecare referrals help people find an appropriate and convenient group.
4. Counseling subjects are introduced to suitable groups.

Chart 25

age, a church also will need geographic divisions. Staff members will spend most of their days in the field, doing visitation with their L's and X's.

By the time a church reaches a size of 10,000, it will assign as many staff to geographic-district work as to age-life stage division work.

Growth need not slow down at 10,000. The Meta-Church can grow to any size without revising its social architecture for ministry or sacrificing quality of discipleship. For the size of harvest now reach- able on Planet Earth, the metamodel is truly the way for pastors to prepare their churches for the future.

Metaglobe Zones for an Office File-Folder System

Use standard colors available from stationary suppliers. Or a ready- to-assemble Meta-file box may be purchased. To inquire about this or other Meta-Church resources, call The Meta-Church Project™ at 1-800- MAP-META, FAX 1-800-289-6129 or FAX 1-818-449-6129.

> Clear—Spirituality Issues
>> Prayer
>> Faith and vision
>> Dysfunctional social systems
> Purple—Governance
>> Head of staff (CEO)
>> Program leadership staff
>> Boards and committees
>>> Agendas
>>> Audit
>>> Budget
>>> Denominational affairs
>>> Membership
>>> Missions
>>> Operations
>>> Personnel
>>> Priorities
>>> Social service and action
>>> Stewardship
>> Planning: Long-range and annual
>>> Goals
>>> Pace and rhythm
>>> Priorities

       Resource allocations
    Budgets (gray)
    Staff issues (use white file folders)
       Compensation and benefits
       Delegation and supervision
       Discipline and termination
       Division of work and position descriptions
       Performance evaluation and professional growth
       Selection and employment
    Lay-ministry development issues (use manila file folders)
    VHS
    Super Bowl recruitment meetings
    Reports
Gray—Finance
  Business
  Construction
  Data processing
    Accounting
    Calendaring
    Electronic mail
    Membership database
    Word processing
  Development
  Duplicating, mailing
  Finance
  Grounds keeping
  Housekeeping
  Maintenance
  Personnel
  Procurement
  Reception
  Scheduling
  Security
  Support staff
Red—Worship Celebration
  Worship services
  Special services for Christmas
  Special services for Easter
  Guest events
  Other plenary events
  Groups (use red or pink file folders)

Platform leadership, order of service, emceeing

Featured talent, guest performers

Technical/production support (audio, video, lights, translation, stage setup)

Audience control (ushering, emergencies, indoor security, offerings)

Audience support (registration, hospitality, health needs, nursery child care)

Traffic, parking supervision, outside security

Talent development issues (use brown file folders)

Guilds, troupes, and forums

Video workshops

Camps

Orange—Auxiliary and Extension

Auxiliary organizations

Auxiliary commercial activities

Auxiliary educational organizations

Direct missions involvement

Extension projects

Financial performance review

General training activities

Yellow—Bridging and Mezzanine

Age-stage divisional programming

Fellowships with acquaintance facilitation

Geographic sector or ZIP/postal-zone programming

Meeting, calendar, interpretation, and facilitation

Advertising (print and electronic)

Direct mail

Handouts

Public relations

Telephoning (in and out)

Master calendar

Newcomer arrangements

New-member arrangements

Seminar events

Special activities

Green—Nurture Groups (light green) and Ministry Teams (dark green)

Ministry teams

Ministry team leader training and supervision

Nurture groups

Nurture group leader training and supervision
VHS coordinating committee
Blue—Telecare/Pastoral Care (light blue) and
Counseling/Support Groups (dark blue)
Clinical counseling
Crisis response teams
Emergency ministry to the needy
Lay counseling
Pastoral care and counseling coordination group
Support groups
Telecare
Walk-in care

11
See Yourself as Manager and Communicator

Imagine that you live in a large metropolis somewhere in the United States or Canada. You attend a church of several thousand. Your pastor is known and discussed throughout the community because of the innovative and sometimes controversial ways he proclaims the good news of Jesus Christ.

A best-selling book contains a chapter featuring your pastor as a leading advocate for a non-Christian religious movement! Book reviewers and other pastors repeat the accusation. Those clergy opposed to your pastor make critical statements in their writings, sermons, and on Christian talk shows. Some of the newer people in your church begin murmuring, "There it is in print, so it must be true. Our pastor must be haywire. And I had placed such a trust in him!"

Problem is, the story was false to begin with. And prior to going to press, no one had consulted your pastor or otherwise verified his communications or beliefs.

He's in town now, but thousands of copies of the misrepresenting book have already been sold. How easy will it be to convey the truth to every active person in your church? What level of communication is necessary in a church to make sure that everyone's hesitations receive an adequate personal response? Will a brief pulpit announcement or a lengthy church newsletter article suffice? Is some other notification system needed?

An analogous situation took place in Los Angeles, where Robert Schuller, Dutch Reformed pastor of the Crystal Cathedral, was accused in a book of being a leading advocate of New Age thought. When Dr. Schuller challenged the editor, the man said, "I'm sorry I didn't check with you, but the book is already released."

Dr. Schuller went before his cell-group leaders and said, "See this book? It's not true! I'm not a New Ager. I don't believe in reincarnation; I don't use quartz crystals; I'm not a vegetarian; and I don't agree with their view of God. Let me explain what I believe, which is orthodox Christian faith." He proceeded to expound on a Reformed theological view of the Christian faith.

After listening to their pastor's personal rebuttal and clarification, no cell leader needed to have a lingering question. But if he or she did, the question could have been put directly to Dr. Schuller himself.

Within two weeks every interested cell-group member could have heard the truth presented in an intimate enough context to allow two-way conversation. Dr. Schuller, a master communicator, had successfully defused a potentially divisive threat. The Crystal Cathedral staff could direct its energies toward more important matters.

A Meta-Church utilizes a similar communications infrastructure. The Meta-Church interior, with its strong cell network and decentralized approach to ministry, is able to be in touch with its senior pastor to maintain strong management and communication no matter how large the church becomes. The purpose of this chapter is to describe how such a system can work.

Flat Organizational Model

A full-scale Meta-Church, even with tens of thousands of people, would, like the Crystal Cathedral, be three-people deep for most downward messaging. From the senior pastor to every small group participant, the hierarchical chart is quite flat: CEO to X to I. For others the organizational model is equally shallow: CEO to C to I. In addition, the senior pastor speaks directly to all I's during the celebration services and to all D's at staff meetings.

The pathway for people-to-pastor communication works almost as easily. Any I's with complaints or questions voice them to their X. Anything resolvable on the cell level is handled on the spot. Otherwise, the issue goes to the L, who responds immediately or carries it to a D. An alternative route is for the X to approach the D directly at the next VHS meeting.

Like the Jethro models described in Chapter 9, the pathway for upward messaging functions are like a decentralized appellate system. Most traffic gets handled with immediacy and personal care between the X's and their I's.

A Bottom-Up Vision of Ministry

The Meta-Church rests on a bottom-up vision of ministry. Everything the church's leadership does provides an organizational climate that supports the grass-roots efforts of the X-led group. The meaningful relationships, support, and love of a nurture cell constitute the church's production center for changed lives. The cell is truly the basic building block of the spiritual community.

What a contrast with the evangelical tradition of "meeting" people to death! In the Baptist circles of my former pastorates, we used the motto, "Three to thrive." We led our people to sit through a Sunday-morning service, then a Sunday-evening service, and then a Wednesday-night meeting. We conditioned our people to do more sitting than ministry!

Increased size seems only to compound the problem. Too many large churches are actually the accumulated graduates of unsuccessful smaller churches. Always 60 percent and commonly up to 90 percent of their alleged new life comes from professing Christians seeking a haven of anonymity where they can take some R and R from burnout at the front lines of smaller churches.

What's the most commonly missing leadership skill whose absence causes this situation to occur? Pastors don't know how to deputize believers for ministry, get reports from them, give them feedback, and reaffirm their vision so that these people keep their ministries effective, motivated, and contributing to the whole. In other words, these con-

Meta-Church Flat
Organization Chart

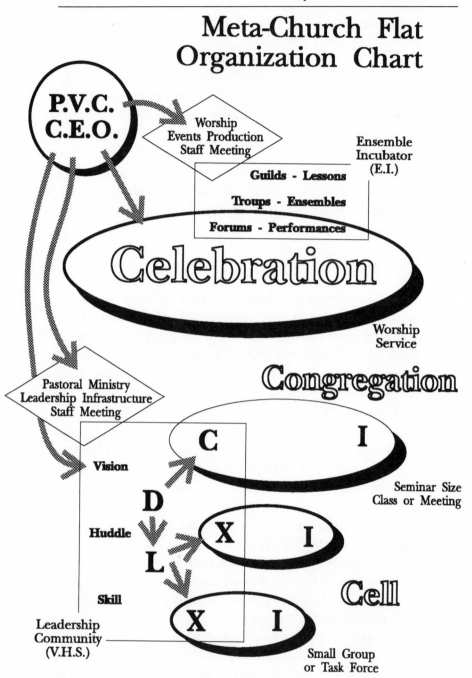

Chart 26

ventionally trained ministers lack the management skills and communication system necessary to develop a network of healthy, multiplying cells.

The Role of the D

The church leader of the future will look more like a music director than a bureaucratic leader. The symphony conductor deals with a large group, but enjoys the assistance of sectional leaders for the strings, woodwinds, brass, and percussion. Within those groups are subleaders represented by the positions of first trumpet, first flutist, and so on. Various sections rehearse separately, and much work goes on outside of the gatherings of the entire orchestra.

That's how a Meta-Church functions. Its decentralization creates a flat organizational chart.

The CEO may be at the top of the structural configuration, but the heartbeat and ministry center of the Meta-Church universe is where the X is. The cell leader is touched on Sundays by the pastor's communication. The vision portion of the VHS meeting focuses especially on the role of the X. All staff and church decisions are made with pre-eminent attention to the health of the cell, for which the X sets the tone. (*See* Chart 26.)

In a large church the senior pastor's position is much like a CEO (chief executive officer) in a business organization. CEO's make only a small percentage of a corporation's decisions. Most CEO's, for example, have a say in, at most, 10 percent of hiring changes. A CEO's major influence comes through *vision casting*.

Similarly, in a Meta-Church, the CEO's greatest resource is the broadcast of vision at worship services, at staff meetings, and at VHS gatherings. The CEO will be concerned that the church's goal imaging is strategic, enabling, empowering, implementable, and sensible. In the church's downward messaging, asks the CEO, do we challenge people to a dream of being part of our changing lives? In particular, how do our corporate conceptualizations affect the X's in their vital role as small-group shepherds?

Upward messaging deals with a different dynamic: loyalty. The ability to speak and have an organization recognize one's concern, take into account his or her circumstances, and offer appropriate feedback determines and builds allegiance to the leadership and structure of a church.

The Meta-Church requires, at most, four dialog links to get from a small-group member to the CEO, as described earlier in this chapter (I to X, X to L, L to D, and D to CEO). In addition, each of these connections is based on a relationship maintained within a manageable span of care.

X leaders receive their primary care from their L's. How often should a Meta-Church's D's meet with the L's? Their times together should be on a personal-appointment basis, according to the L's level of maturity, but not less often than monthly.

When a Meta-Church is young, D's will meet with their L's every two weeks—the same frequency as the VHS meeting. As an L matures, monthly meetings will probably be adequate. Later, as a Meta-Church needs to develop geographic districts (see Chapter 10), the D's will spend much of their time in the field, visiting one-on-one with their L's and traveling with the L's to meet with X's.

Policy Hats Versus Ministry Hats

One of the difficulties faced by a church of 1,000 in average attendance at worship or a church just broaching the 800–1,000 barrier is the need to separate the roles of those sitting on the board from their roles as volunteer leaders within the ministry organization. While the board may set policy, endorse plans and budgets, and audit compliance, the senior pastor must behave as head of staff and accept responsibility for the overall guidance of the volunteer networks.

In essence, the shift necessary at the 1,000 threshold is from a board-led church to a staff-led church. The senior pastor must therefore accept a CEO title and responsibility for the supervision of staff and the carrying out of objectives. A senior pastor who shows reluctance in accepting this responsibility will limit the development of the church. It's the CEO's vision casting and his or her leadership through paid staff that generally facilitate the ongoing growth of this size church.

Occasionally, a board member might double as a volunteer staff member in the area of executive function, but such an exception is usually temporary. Board members with that capability are usually too busy in the business world to give a church priority at the time and with the reliability needed for a staff position.

The senior pastor may hire an executive pastor to help him handle personnel and coordination issues for the staff. But how that executive is used will vary depending on personality, gift mix, delegation training, and other factors. The executive pastor will be coordinator and thus "more equal" than the other D's.

Each of these D's on staff will have ministry organizations of volunteers that are charted below them. The crucial issue is that staff discern between what is the policy-setting governing board and what is the ministry organization of volunteers.

Governing boards have one primary ministry: dealing with policy. That can occur both sitting around a table and praying on one's knees beside that table. Then, as board members leave the room, they must remove their policy hats and don the hats appropriate for whatever roles they play as participants in the ministry organization. (*See* Chart 27.)

In the small church, policy and ministry mesh closely because the governing board is also the operating and management committee for the church. Someone sits at the board-room table because he or she leads a particular ministry—or vice versa.

Smaller churches therefore find it difficult to define the difference between policy and operation. Churches unable to distinguish between policy and operational matters are generally still too small to worry about the issue!

By the time a church reaches 1,000, board agendas will be too long, if the staff hasn't weeded out the operational matters. Those on the board with management skills will say, "Why didn't the staff take care of this? Take it off the agenda," or, "Either bring us an actionable recommendation or build it into the annual plan."

Once a policy is separated from ministry, church staff will have a space in which to work! Creating and maintaining that open spot is a difficult and painful transition for staff and board members alike.

Most denominations established their policy at a time when virtually all of their churches were 200 or fewer in size. Larger, growing churches, therefore, sometimes feel frustrated with their denomination's recommended governing machinery.

Changing Roles of Boards, Staff and Ministers

Beyond 800,
New Roles for Staff

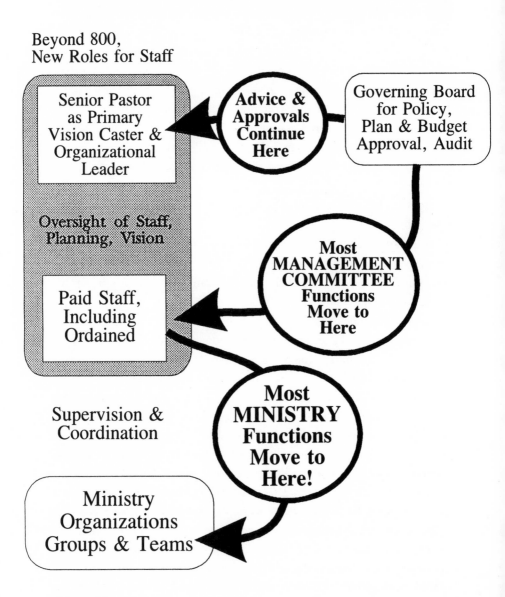

Senior Pastor
as Primary
Vision Caster &
Organizational
Leader

Advice &
Approvals
Continue
Here

Governing Board
for Policy,
Plan & Budget
Approval, Audit

Oversight of Staff,
Planning, Vision

Paid Staff,
Including
Ordained

Most
MANAGEMENT
COMMITTEE
Functions
Move to
Here

Supervision &
Coordination

Most
MINISTRY
Functions
Move to
Here!

Ministry
Organizations
Groups & Teams

Chart 27

The entire Free Methodist denomination, for example, contains only a few churches with weekly attendances of 600 or more. Pastor Gary Walsh, of Pearce Memorial Church near Rochester, New York, wanted to change the order so his church could more easily expand to large-church status. He spoke with his bishop, who with the concurrence of another bishop relaxed certain rules to encourage experimenting with certain structural innovations. The two of them next asked their Quadrennial Conference to sanction these organizational changes. The conference said, in effect, that if church structure is impeding this church's progress, it's probably hurting others as well. So the Quadrennial Conference took the unexpected step of granting the freedom to innovate to every church in the denomination! That's courageous.

Decentralize Almost Everything

As churches modify their structures to be more progressive and staff led, the immediate danger is that the paid clergy will revert to doing the ministry as the ministers. Rather, every pastor and paid church staff should sum up each week's activities by asking, ''To what extent did I contribute to the making of ministers who care for our constituency and those beyond our constituency in the name of Jesus Christ?'' That standard of measurement will result in much decentralization, even in the areas of evangelism, assimilation, apprentice making, and crisis coping.

Evangelism. Most churches tend to centralize their evangelism. They train certain task forces to serve as their search-and-kill teams. This equipping idea is excellent, but the format can easily bottleneck the greater work that God might choose to do.

Granted, Evangelism Explosion trained squads and other specialized crews accomplish far more than a church with no outreach strategy. But they may resemble more the single mouth of one dinosaur than the innumerable mouths of a metropoliswide convention of mice. In a race to eat a mountain of grain, who could do a better job: a one-ton brontosaurus or a ton of rodents? (*See* Chapter 3 for the basis of this dinosaur-mouse comparison.)

Why not instead outfit every small-group leader with the skills of an Evangelism Explosion worker (or some equivalent)? Evangelization will then occur at the level of every cell, rather than at some place remote from most people of the church.

After all, effective evangelism has both social and spiritual aspects. The ability to hear the gospel is sometimes enhanced by a sense of acceptance from the evangelizer (*see* Chapter 5). The life of Christ in a loving cell group may be presented so attractively and powerfully that conversions may occur even without formal soul-winning skills on the part of the leader!

Someone may join a cell and four months later report, "I met God this week." Everyone asks, "How? Nobody here explained the plan of salvation." The person answers, "In desperation, I got on my knees and said 'O God, help!' I've always felt accepted by this group; now I sense an acceptance by God." There was an experience of conversion! Now the group must help the new believer put a theological form around his or her experience.

Assimilation. Many churches follow a pastor's-class, sponsor-family, or otherwise centralized model of helping new people feel at home. What if that responsibility shifted to the cell groups? What if every ten-person group saw itself as the initial pastor's class and sponsoring family? Assimilation would be more personalized, more spontaneous, and more widespread. Plus, people who link relationally to a church through one of its small units don't fall through the cracks when it comes to the large units, such as the worship celebration.

Whenever a church says, "We have an assimilation problem," it's acknowledging itself as a front-door church. Even the most effective side-door church will have front-door visitors. Churches need a centralized program to keep such visitors from walking in the front door and out the back. But as much as possible, churches will look to the cells as binding social contexts for newcomers.

Apprentice Development. When decentralization occurs, the central church is no longer responsible for creating the emerging leadership needed for new cells. Traditional means simply cannot recruit and provide enough leaders. Even if they could, processing potential leaders in classes is inferior to one-on-one apprenticeship. Nothing can be more personalized than an X nurturing his or her Xa until that Xa reaches the level of practice required to be an effective X.

How long will someone remain in apprenticeship training? Based on the maturity of the trainee, the process may take from four months to two years. Some timid souls will need even longer.

Even so, when a church has 50 to 100 cell ministries competing for available future leaders, and the senior leadership is casting a vision for doubling, a major problem can be brewing! In a centralized system, people are desperately scanning computer lists and talking on the phone at all hours. They receive a lot of no answers from parishioners who think, *I don't really know this caller. Besides, she's got fifty more households she can contact. Let someone else try that ministry.*

By contrast, the feeling at the cell level would be: "It's one of us, folks." Small groups become breeder units for creating new leaders.

What if such a system creates more torchbearers than it currently needs? After all, individual mentoring, when multiplied by the number of existing cells, means that the leadership core will soon double in size.

A church must develop "extra" leadership, or its quality will deteriorate. Every successful corporation creates leader–managers faster than they're usable. In kingdom work, however, harvest laborers are always in demand (Matthew 9:37, 38). It would seem that God sends a church about as many people to care for as it is willing to provide trained leaders to handle them.

When churches commission deputized, badge-carrying cell-group leaders with the job of finding and recruiting their own people, they will do so until there are few uncared-for church members. But if the number of leaders is right, everybody gets care with a depth not possible in a system of assigning people to lists from a central computer database.

Crisis Coping. Everyone experiences an occasional crisis—from the death of a loved one to a personal trauma like bankruptcy or divorce. Any church that hopes to give people the long-term support they really need must involve nurture cells as part of its decentralized care system. A new widow, for example, will need an unwinding period of two years for her grief. The self-care compact of a healthy cell can bolster her in ways not feasible for the church that has only a few primary care providers, the professional clergy.

Every Sized Church

Whether a church is a cat-size fellowship of fifty or a beyond-huge, metropoliswide gathering of mice, its CEO's overriding message will still be directed at the X, saying "Bless you, because you are the key to everything. Don't call the church staff first. We're always available for backup work, coaching work, and referral work. God will use *you*. You lay hands on the sick. You prepare them to receive the blessings of the Spirit of God."

Any pastor and any church can, from day one, project that vision. I consult with churches new and old, little and big. The metamodel provides all of them with a big-picture approach to directing ministry.

It doesn't surprise me that many of the early adopter churches are at the 1,000 barrier. That's the transitional window most motivated by pain! At that point, pastors must make some changes or die. Traditional solutions will remove administrative pressures; the Meta-Church system designs changes that take ceilings off growth.

Is there a need in the metasystem for planting new churches? In most circumstances, it's a must! The wise pastor will lead a church in a constant rhythm of expanding, then extending, then expanding, then extending. Without both, a church typically invites a lot of heartache.

In many cases, the mother church benefits so much from the "daughtering" that in two years' time it's both rebuilt and healthier—even if it sent out key leaders. Large churches usually have many people who haven't found a place of meaningful service because someone else is sitting in that slot! If you don't extend, you don't have a chance to upwardly develop your people. High-performance Christians will drift off to look for opportunities elsewhere.

What about already-existing smaller and newer churches? Unfortunately, pastors in churches of less than 200 are often so in love with providing primary care to their sheep that they can't bear to turn them loose. Until these shepherds learn to measure their worth in different terms than those to which they've been accustomed, they won't radically empower cell leaders. They'll remain content to let their sheep pay them to minister.

Those pastoring churches of 500 or more are likelier to demonstrate the commitment and ability necessary to delegate ministry to cell-group leaders. These "ranchers" make the best candidates for a successful metamodel transition.

I am convinced more than ever that the Meta-Church offers a manager's and communicator's perspective viable for any church of any size. It repeats a basic biblical question of training, found in 2 Timothy 2:2 and elsewhere: Am I doing the ministry myself, or am I committing others to do it?

If I want the latter to be my answer, what management structure sees to it that churches have a proliferation of ministry-centered nurture cells? Metachurch theory teaches that the central leadership task of the church, after hearing from God, is the development of laypeople who can minister the grace of God in its many forms and, as a result, create obedient disciples of Jesus Christ who apply the truths of the Bible to their everyday lives.

Church infrastructures do not simply happen. The McDonald's hamburger chain can deliver a piping hot Quarter Pounder in less than one minute at the counter only because of a methodology it has fervently, consistently, and intentionally orchestrated. Its most critical person isn't the manager, but the minimum-wage teenager, man, or woman who has been trained in how to get that fresh hamburger to the customer. An entire system, involving millions of dollars of research and thousands of careers, has been coordinated and focused on making that one transaction between customer and counter person successful. If the last person to handle a customer's order fails to perform his or her task, the entire franchise chain's plan for service is torpedoed.

The significant church of the future is one that utilizes nonclergy leadership as the primary medium through which the gospel is propagated and the whole organization of staff and lay leaders as the means by which one hungry person is helped by a small group of others. In other words, the church of the future will embark on a revolution in how its "business" is perceived. Radical changes must occur at every level if lay ministers of home-care groups are to be effective and supported in their work.

I firmly believe that the God of creation has a better plan for the health and wholeness of His people than the traditional church is currently delivering. I have seen that dramatic transformation occur as pastors in every size church organize their life, time, and vision around those activities that produce lay ministers.

The organized church is facing a decade of opportunity. I want to be part of enabling our churches which resemble warehouses of underused Christians to become centers of caring and evangelizing!

Role Descriptions[1]

Minimum functional requirements for metasystem maintenance.

  I. Senior Pastor (CEO)

    A. Cast vision at various combined leaders' meeting (VHS).

    B. Assure D's that ministry community priorities will be maintained.

 II. Full-time Staff Pastors (D's)

    A. Coordinate program planning with master calendar.

    B. Assure that L's are recruiting apprentices.

    C. Assure that L's are assisting cell mitosis after discovering apprentices.

    D. Assure that C's and L's are developing apprentices.

    E. Ensure reporting of group statistics.

    F. Link C's and L's to senior staff.

    G. Initiate Grand Home Visitation, semi-annually.

III. Leaders of Congregation-Size Groups (C's)

    (Mostly volunteers; sometimes part-time staff; occasionally full-time staff.)

    A. Assure performance of X's by creating attraction events.

    B. Assist those X's who lead concern groups to get acquainted with prospective recruits.

    C. Participate in VHS training and worship celebration.

 IV. Coaches of Cell Leaders (L's)

    A. Work closely with D's to provide role support for X's.

    B. Support X's performance in identifying and empowering apprentices.

    C. Link X's with C's and D's.

    D. Keep D's abreast of strengths and problems in groups.

    E. Assist X's in preparing for cell mitosis as apprentices develop.

    F. Maintain a span-of-care of less than a one-to-five ratio by developing La's.

    G. Maintain group meeting sizes that average ten or fewer.

    H. Visit group meetings; conduct feedback sessions with X's and Xa's.

    I. Monitor group financial giving; monitor participation in training and worship events.

    J. Substitute for X's in groups, where appropriate.

    K. Participate in VHS training and worship celebration.

    L. Model group leadership skills for X's in the context of the VHS group.

    M. Help X's deal with or refer EGR's.

    N. Be alert to attitude problems and teaching that's contrary or divisive.

    O. Be alert to attitude problems and to teaching that is contrary or divisive.

    P. Accompany D's and X's on Grand Home Visitation as much as possible.

V. Cell-Group Leaders, Nurture and Task Focus (X's)

    A. Attend VHS meeting and worship celebration.

    B. Make time for feedback sessions with L's.

    C. Watch for emergence of assistant/apprentice leaders.

    D. Report group progress and individual attendance status.

    E. Convene group one to three times a month.

    F. Pray and prepare for group meetings.

    G. Link I's with L's, C's, and D's.

    H. Recruit a host/ess, when appropriate, to see that child care and refreshments are available and venue is arranged.

    I. Pray for spiritual growth and protection of each I.

    J. Notify pastoral staff of acute crisis conditions requiring staff response.

    K. Assure redemptive agenda via Scripture, sharing, prayers, songs, and worship.

    L. Refrain from divisiveness or teaching contrary to church position.

    M. Maintain atmosphere in which all I's discover and develop God-given spiritual gifts.

    N. Refer counseling cases that exceed experience level.

    O. Accept responsibility for new conversion growth by using empty-chair strategy and other effective means.

    P. Lead an exemplary life.

    Q. Surrender token of appointment (identification badge?) if requested, accepting a furlough from leading until issues can be resolved.

    R. Accompany D's and L's on Grand Home Visitation as much as possible.

VI. Cell-Group Participants (I's)

    A. Attend cell meetings.

B. Encourage those present.
C. Experiment to discover spiritual gifts.
D. Discover spiritual direction.
E. Be open for training in group-management skills.
F. Seek a church ministry activity.
G. Be willing to consider serving as an apprentice group leader.
H. Bring friends and seekers.
 I. Share in hospitality and child-care arrangements from time to time, as needed.
J. Give to the general budget of the church.
K. Participate in worship in the celebration service at church.

SECTION V

Where to Go From Here

12
Glean Insights From Others

This chapter profiles three churches, each in a different phase of Meta-Church maturity. I selected newer churches, since their growth patterns are easier to isolate and describe. Each senior pastor, however, received his spiritual formation in a traditional church setting and thus needed to change his perception of ministry to that of a Meta-Church. Then each of these strong leaders faced the challenge of guiding his young church to do likewise.

Conventional churches, led by either new or veteran pastors, are likewise making the transition to Meta-Church philosophy. Because of the many specialized dynamics involved, their stories will have to wait for more extended chronicling in another volume. Chapter 13 and the Bibliography of this book list the resources now available to guide existing churches into Meta-Church growth.

An Exciting Place to Be

Corona, Queens, located two miles southeast of LaGuardia Airport, is part of the urban sprawl known as New York City. A two-block section along National Street boasts a rapidly growing 300-member mosque, a 700-member Kingdom Hall of Jehovah's Witnesses, a Hispanic voodoo priest, an orange-robed Hindu sect, and a 100-year-old, wood-framed, stained-glass-windowed evangelical church building.

The second-floor sanctuary of this building seats 250, but attendance in recent years has averaged fewer than twenty. Worshipers are mostly gray-haired Caucasians who love God but aren't making much of an impact on this neighborhood. They are host to Reverend Scazzero's new mission.

Some half a million people live within a half mile of this block, almost 50 percent of whom are Hispanic. Another sizable portion is Asian. A ten-mile radius encompasses 6.5 million people, representing practically every nation, tongue, and religion on Earth!

The real action in this church building takes place not in the near-vacant sanctuary, but downstairs, in the first-floor social hall. Its fluorescent lights, folding chairs, and makeshift stage house hundreds of people every Sunday for the 9:00 A.M. (English), 11:15 A.M. (English) or 1:15 P.M. (Spanish) services of New Life Fellowship, begun in 1987, using features of the Meta-Church model as its guiding philosophy.

The Pastor. Pete Scazzero, who at age thirty-one founded the church, was born into an Italian Catholic home and came to a personal faith in Christ during college. He credits his spiritual formation to years spent with Inter-Varsity Christian Fellowship, first as a student and then as a full-time staff member.

After three years on IVCF staff, he enrolled in a seminary. During his final year of study, Scazzero sought the Lord about the future. "God gave me a vision for the establishing of a large, citywide church, coupled with a mandate to learn Spanish!" he says.

As a result, six weeks after graduating, Scazzero and his new bride, also a former IVCF staff member, boarded a plane to Costa Rica, where their denomination, the Christian and Missionary Alliance, funded a year of language study. Their bilingual skills then equipped them to come to New York to serve on staff at a Hispanic church and teach at a Spanish Bible institute.

"During that year I also waited on the Lord," says Pete Scazzero. "God clarified His initial call to New York City, saying that I was to plant a church in two languages, based on home cells that would extend throughout the five boroughs and reach an attendance into the thousands.''

Change of Strategy. The first attempt at planting a church failed. Pastor Scazzero had, through prayer and fasting, begun a fruitful street evangelism, a variety of evangelistic Bible studies with non-Christians, and discipleship-oriented studies with unchurched Christians who were looking for a spiritual family. He gradually gathered an initial team of about fifty for the beginning of services in early 1987.

''About six weeks into this first attempt, I realized we were in big trouble,'' reflects Pastor Scazzero. ''We had few stable people, because I had tried to build the church primarily with those touched by my street witnessing. We met on Sunday nights in a crime-ridden neighborhood in an old school auditorium that seats 554. Unfortunately, we had only 20!''

Pastor Scazzero believes that God used the circumstances to break his sense of self-sufficiency. ''I was totally depleted, knowing my back was against the wall. So this first church wasn't really a failure.''

The next week, armed with mountain-moving faith, Pastor Scazzero met with C. Peter Wagner at a conference sponsored by the Charles E. Fuller Institute of Evangelism and Church Growth (which will be described further in Chapter 13). ''Dr. Wagner told me that anyone trying to plant a church in New York City without a team was on a suicide run,'' reflects Pastor Scazzero. ''I could believe him!''

Wagner advised the young minister to adopt a different strategy for church planting by doing four things: Start again with a core group of at least fifty; pray for God to bring unchurched *believers* who were looking for a church home; pray and fast until he found a usable and affordable building for Sunday-morning worship; and select a new name for the church. ''In less than three months, God miraculously answered all four prayers,'' says Pastor Scazzero.

In September, 1987, New Life started over, strong, with an enthusiastic worship service and an obvious passion for outreach. The idea spread like wildfire. As parishioners invited their friends and neighbors to this exciting new church, Pastor Scazzero encouraged them to participate in home Bible studies.

At first, he headed all the groups himself (mainly English language, with a few in Spanish). He followed the format he learned in his university days and as a staff member with IVCF: worship, inductive Bible study, prayer, fellowship, and evangelism.

As soon as possible, however, he began passing cell-group leadership to the skilled, mature laypeople whom he had attracted to his core. Most of these key people were already overseeing a specific emphasis: music, youth, children, internationals, Hispanics (including Spanish-language meetings on Friday nights), or prayer. Thus the ministry leaders, acting also as cell-group leaders, formed a strong backbone for the fledgling church.

New Life developed cell groups throughout diverse areas of the city, from the war-torn ghettos of the South Bronx to Manhattan to Brooklyn to, naturally, Queens. "While Corona is our celebration locale, we see ourselves as a regional church with people coming from all over New York City, Long Island, and even New Jersey," says Pastor Scazzero.

VHS Meetings. By this time Pastor Scazzero had received consultation about metagrowth principles. Using his catalytic personality and confident, secure faith, he rallied his leadership around the Meta-Church recommended system of bimonthly VHS meetings (*see* Chapter 9). These became the foundation for training and motivating his leadership. He realized that for ongoing growth, New Life must maintain quality in its discipleship, breed new leadership, and multiply its number of home cells.

As the waves of newcomers kept rolling in, New Life kept pace by providing opportunities for their nurture and involvement. By mid 1991 combined attendance at the Sunday worship celebrations averaged 520, and the number of home-cell groups exceeded 50.

What, from the human perspective, sustains New Life's growth rate? Friendship evangelism, fishing ponds, and cells bring guests through the side door, while radio and other advertising draw through the front door. (Chapter 5 explains this "door" terminology.)

Many of the newcomers stay because they find the worship— especially the music and the use of spiritual gifts—festive and contemporary, the preaching powerful and relevant, the cell groups caring, and the opportunities for leadership development abundant. They sense an acceptance, an attractive vision, and a momentum as part of a great work of God. New Life, under the dynamic leadership of Pete Scazzero, is an exciting place to be!

The ethnic diversity of the greater community parallels the makeup of New Life: Hispanic (30 percent), Asian and International (30 percent), Anglo (20 percent), Afro-American/West Indian (15 percent), and other (5 percent). Interestingly, but not surprisingly, the cell groups tend to remain homogenous. Some are largely Filipino, others Hispanic (either English- or Spanish-language), another predominantly single people, another with married couples, and so on.

Difficulties. However, even a church with a delightful 80 percent annual growth rate can face staggering problems. The typical blue-collar, lower- or lower-middle-class parishioner gives a proportionally small amount of his or her income to the church. The worship room is packed to the point of sociological strangulation, bathrooms are inadequate, and the children's classrooms and nursery are overcrowded. New Life desperately needs additional programming for youth and children. It must also find more full-time staff members, particularly ethnic ones. The present structure lacks administrative organizers and policy-making boards.

One day New Life will establish a formal membership, require its leaders to affirm certain doctrinal particulars (at present X's and Xa's must "be committed to the vision of New Life and be loyal to her leadership"), and set up an accountability structure for its senior leadership. Meanwhile, however, the church plows ahead in ministry!

Philosophy of Ministry. "The needs in an urban community like New York are overwhelming," says Pastor Scazzero. "Drugs, poverty, AIDS, intense spiritual warfare, and droves of unstable, dysfunctional people—it's hard to comprehend. I've learned to see the City as a frontier to conquer, not as a jungle from which to flee."

How does he keep the church headed forward? "I'm a trainer of leadership, not a primary caregiver," he says. "Vision casting is my number-one job. I make sure to spend the majority of my time in prayer, in the Word, and in developing leadership."

Pastor Scazzero realizes that no magic formula can produce instant leaders. "Our future growth is limited by our leadership," he says. "Give me ten solid cell-group leaders, and our attendance will grow by another 100, because we'll have provided an environment where the Holy Spirit's gifts can be released to do the work of ministry."

Next Steps. New Life's initial echelon of mature leaders, who like Pastor Scazzero arrived at the church with a commitment to friendship evangelism and small-group ministry, are now L's (coaches of five cell leaders). One is a D (pastoral staff member who supervises several L's). Approximately two thirds of the small-group shepherds are women.

Several of the cell-group leaders (X's) and apprentices (Xa's) are new Christians. "Young Christians who lead cell groups grow like crazy," comments Pastor Scazzero, "especially as they learn to base their identity in Christ instead of in their ministries or on their egos."

As these young leaders receive assistance and supervision, the church must also cultivate new Xa's and advance the current X's into new groups or to the L level.

Pastor Scazzero represents the kind of leader who knows the next step God has for his flock. He also realizes the challenges of discipling his sizable church. "Lots of our people enter through the front door," he explains. "We struggle to direct them into home groups. If they don't get into a cell, generally they leave because they don't develop relationships."

By contrast, "If someone comes into the church through the side door of a small group," says Pastor Scazzero, "they need no special followup. They're as good as in the church!"

Clearly the hand of the Lord has guided the explosive beginning of New Life. At present a healthy 80 percent of the church attends both cell-group and Sunday-worship celebration, and both these segments of the church are multiplying in number.

As potential obstacles to ministry continue to be overcome, the growth potential of this Meta-Church will remain virtually unlimited.

From "Hunting-License Issuer" to "Bait Cutter"

Grace Fellowship Church, Baltimore, Maryland, began in 1980 with six couples committed to several core values, including the value and primacy of small groups. One of the cofounding pastors, twenty-seven-year-old Reverend Jim Dethmer, had received his training from a traditional evangelical seminary and then served on the staff of a Bible church in Texas.

In Grace's seventh year, Pastor Dethmer embarked on a journey that would move it from being a church *with* small groups to becoming a

Meta-Church *based on* nurturing cells. By 1990 attendance was averaging 1,400. Pastor Dethmer believes God used the church's reshaped
direction to develop that kind of growth.

Pastor Dethmer first heard of Meta-Church principles at a Charles E.
Fuller Institute seminar in Anderson, Indiana. As he, Bob Logan (a
church-planting pastor who had founded Community Baptist Church,
in Alta Loma, California, and had helped to pioneer Meta-Church
ideas before leaving that post), and I walked across a field of dande-
lions, I plucked one and blew on its tuft. We watched the feathery
seeds scatter in every direction, and I said, "This is what the infrastructure of the church of the future will be like. Cell groups grow,
birth, disperse, and create a whole field of new life. Nothing will keep
them from spreading."

Introducing the Idea. The dandelion analogy of a lay-driven cell
ministry captured Pastor Dethmer's imagination. We conversed about
the Meta-Church idea for hours. Then he returned home, met with his
elders, and over time presented a vision of Grace Fellowship Church
linked to an explosion of unstoppable growth. He developed an acros-
tic for the concept:

> **M** stands for *multiplying cells* through a structure that builds
> quantity without sacrificing quality.
>
> **E** stands for *empowering laypeople* through a gift-based, decen-
> tralized, "yes"-oriented ministry system. Empowerment
> takes place through equipping and enabling.
>
> **T** stands for *training leaders and apprentices* through a VHS
> system of leadership community meetings.
>
> **A** stands for *adoring God* through the metaglobe's upper hemi-
> sphere concept of festive celebration.

Grace's leadership liked the Meta-Church idea. Many of them, like
Pastor Dethmer, had backgrounds with Campus Crusade for Christ,
Young Life, Navigators, or Inter-Varsity Christian Fellowship. Thus
they had come to Grace committed to the importance of small-group
discipleship and were skilled in how to lead and coach such groups.

Further, a high percentage of Grace's laypeople were already involved in a group. For someone to become a church member, for
example, one of four required commitments was to join a small group.

These groups played a prominent role in church life, particularly since Pastor Dethmer had intentionally avoided establishing Sunday- and Wednesday-night services, as well as other major weeknight programs.

Even with all these positive developments already in place, Pastor Dethmer still needed to use his strong leadership abilities and vision-casting pulpit skills to guide Grace across a number of hurdles for it to become a Meta-Church.

New Mind-set. First, both pastor and people had to change certain attitudes. During Pastor Dethmer's seminary training, he had been trained to believe the assumption that the most important event in the life of a church is its large-group celebration. Therefore, he concluded, the most important person in the church is the one who officiates at that gathering. What role can be more important than guiding a worship service so that people can touch God through the communication of the Word, through song, and through corporate prayer?

The Meta-Church, with its emphasis on discipleship, stresses just the opposite. Where does the most life change occur? In what context do people become conformed to the image of the Lord Jesus Christ? Experience indicates that these transformations occur best in small groups. There believers can experience transparency, vulnerability, listening, and use of spiritual gifts one to another. People get involved, and bench warming becomes minimized.

If the preacher or worship leader isn't the church VIP, then who is? The lay shepherds who lead the house churches! "In the Meta-Church," says Pastor Dethmer, "the small-group shepherd fishes, and everybody else cuts bait." He emphasizes the importance of his X's with a sketch of them standing waist-high in fishing waders, while other church leaders (the D's, C's, and L's) bring them bait. "The reason we exist is to make small-group leaders successful in fishing," he says.

He emphasizes the pivotal role of his X's through how he introduces his sermon illustrations ("I was talking with one of our shepherds the other day and . . ."), how much effort he puts into preparing for the vision section of the VHS meetings, how his reports to his board carefully balance southern and northern hemispheres, and how, in his one-on-one appointments, he insists that the counselee bring his or her X to the meeting. "These decisions help us authenticate our X's and recognize them as the champions that they are," he says.

It took Pastor Dethmer several years to undergo an attitude reversal in his inmost self. He now believes that the most important people in a church are the small-group leaders.

He affirms that the all-congregation celebrations, as they create an atmosphere conducive for people to touch God, should support and reinforce what takes place in the small groups—rather than vice versa. "Most senior pastors will find it easier to install the technology of the Meta-Church system than to experience a true change of mind," he warns.

In fact, one of the questions regularly asked of cell leaders was: "What are we doing to communicate (a) that you're the most important person in this church or (b) that you're *not* the most important person?"

Predictably, the answers to that inquiry led to some major adjustments! For example, decision making used to be an elder-led, top-down approach. Now the small-group shepherds have a greater say. They also play a role in the process of disseminating information.

Or the church previously tended to say "no" to creative requests suggested by the cell groups. Today the church allows far more flexibility in the what, when, where, how, and with whom of cell ministry. The church leadership has established the why: Small groups are to grow through personal life change and through inviting acquaintances as new members. Each leader is free to determine the meeting time and place, the group constituency, and the balance of love, learn, decide, and do (Chapter 6 explains these latter four terms).

Leaders report group dynamics on their monthly forms at the VHS meetings. "We try to authenticate the significance of our X's by almost never saying no," says Pastor Dethmer. "One of the keys to making heroes of people, which is what we want to do with our X's, is to say yes to their visions, their dreams, and their ideas."

Reducing Mass. Grace's second hurdle in its conversion to a Meta-Church dealt with small-group size, which at that time ranged from twelve to twenty-five. The largeness hampered attempts at care and nurture. It did allow, however, a heavy emphasis on learning. The pastoral team had developed its own small-group curriculum, designed to dovetail with the Sunday sermon.

Just as decentralization shifted agenda decisions to the small groups themselves, so the church staff allowed each group to reach its own conclusion about reducing its size. The staff taught about the operations of small-group health. "Most of our leaders realized that the values that had drawn their group together and created its synergistic camaraderie would be snuffed out if the group exceeded a certain size and continued in that 'overweight' condition," says Pastor Dethmer.

A few groups, aware of the indicators of group death, retained their large size and eventually dissolved.

Most others, through a daughtering process, formed subgroups. These progeny came to life as Pastor Dethmer and his staff cast the vision for birthing and groomed certain skills in the X's.

They, in turn, discovered and developed apprentices (Xa's), who could lead the new cells. Finally, the actual transition occurred as the twelve- to twenty-five-person groups began clustering into subgroups of four to eight for a significant portion of their typical meetings.

Within a year, all church groups had twelve or fewer people.

Opening Closed Groups. The third and most difficult hurdle to jump involved the closed nature of all the existing small groups. The underlying assumption was that people would be transparent and vulnerable before God and each other only within "safe" settings—meaning closed groups. For several years Grace had followed the pattern of organizing house churches, as they were called, in September, terminating them in June, and then reshuffling everyone in September.

In keeping with the "yes" system of sensitivity to small-group leaders, church staff proposed the change as a *suggestion*. As with the issue of reducing group size, cell leaders received teaching about the dangers of keeping their groups closed. A few long-time group leaders added persuasive testimonies concerning how their groups had died for lack of new life. Soon the majority of lay shepherds decided to welcome newcomers to their groups.

Most groups opted to open slowly. They each set certain dates, every four to six weeks, when members could bring guests. They also encouraged their members to voice any fears about strangers' destroying the intimacy level of their group.

As the transition occurred, many groups discovered that new people, if properly brought on board through appropriate questions and appreciative listening, accentuate the feeling of intimacy!

"A trademark of a dying group is boredom, because everybody chews on the same old food," explains Pastor Dethmer. "Newcomers bring fun, zest, and vitality. Each person in the group gets to tell his or her life story again, which everyone loves doing. New people present provide an excuse for doing so!"

By 1990, Grace Fellowship Church sponsored about seventy adult small groups, 90 percent of which were unrestricted. Of the remaining 10 percent, several involved therapeutic issues and healing opportunities for EGR's ("extra grace required" believers, described in Chapters 7 and 8). A handful of others remained unnecessarily closed. Most of these are, unfortunately, ebbing away into a slow death.

Balancing Span of Care. A final and ongoing stage in Grace Fellowship Church's transformation involves its structure for leadership support. The previous system of one staff member overseeing all the small groups (thirty-seven at one point!) created obvious span-of-care difficulties for both this pastor and his leaders.

Further, no decentralizing impetus urged anyone to generate new groups. All the organization came from the top down.

As one outworking of this original system, the church followed an inconsistent and unintentional approach to leadership development—a hunting-license approach. "Do you want to be a small group leader? Great! Here's the curriculum. Go get 'em." Some men and women succeeded, especially when the church was still small enough for them to maintain informal contact with Grace's senior leadership.

But as the church grew, so did the burnout rate. With no VHS system, leaders would serve a year or two and then take off the next four until they recovered from a "never again" mentality.

The system also offered no incentive for participants to invite their neighbors. All the groups were front-door created, rather than side-door assimilated. People who attended the worship service (northern hemisphere on the metaglobe) would be invited to a new-member class (which served as the mezzanine). From here they received assignment to a small group.

The structure didn't allow for "fishing." Assimilation and social binding took place within each group *after* its assignees had reported for meetings.

True, Grace's cell system was built on several healthy practices.

For example, lay-led teams decentralized the hospital-visitation portion of pastoral care. The church even decentralized Holy Communion and baptism to the cell-group level. (As churches, even old-line liturgical ones, search through their history, they often discover that it's not so much their theology or tradition as their clergy that prevent flexibility in administering the sacraments!)

But certain liabilities needed to be addressed. As a first step toward a solution, Pastor Dethmer highlighted his dream regarding the need for L's. He explained the reason X's and D's burn out, and he described how L's could make a significant difference through their skills in diagnosing problems, managing crises, and debugging dysfunctional groups.

The church staff carefully selected a number of potential L's and asked them to serve in that capacity for six months. About 80 percent proved successful and continued on as L's.

Next, Pastor Dethmer distinguished the role of C's from that of L's and X's. "C's, like outdoor bug lights, can draw a crowd. They have a God-given ability to attract people," says Pastor Dethmer. The net result is that C's create fishing ponds (*see* Chapter 10 for an introduction to this congregation-size bridging concept).

In its early stages, a Meta-Church can grow without fishing ponds. Until 75 percent or more of the church has joined a small group, most X's and Xa's can find fish—new people to invite to their group—within easy reach.

The role of C's becomes vital when a church has developed so much leadership that they must beat the bushes to uncover potential cell members. Grace Fellowship Church began reaching this phase in its third year of Meta-Church development.

Vision, Huddle, and Skill. In the meanwhile, the pastors inaugurated a VHS system, which they term Leadership Community Meeting, for developing the C's, L's, X's, and apprentices.

The leaders gained much from this constant exposure to the vision of the church. "When ministry is radically decentralized, people begin to wonder how they make a difference to the whole," says Pastor Dethmer. "Vision casting constantly communicates why they're so significant to the movement of God in this community."

Pastor Dethmer enjoys the privilege of watching his people unite around the vision of their church. "Most churches gather their key movers and shakers only once or twice a year, such as at a leadership retreat. Our Leadership Community Meetings provide me with first-hand exposure to the opinion leaders in our church twice a month. I consider my twenty- to thirty-minute opportunities for vision casting to be my central speaking engagement—more important, even, than my Sunday-morning preaching!"

Prayer is a core value in the vision-casting process. "I like the metaglobe idea of a prayer atmosphere," he says. "The air around us may be invisible, but it's essential. I'm convinced that without a prayer canopy in a Meta-Church, the pastor will end up with nothing more than a well-organized opportunity for the flesh to flourish."

In recent years, Pastor Dethmer has begun reading solid books on prayer, journaling, and spending extended times in solitude, silence, and fasting. "I can't go without it, or our whole church becomes vulnerable," he says. "Prayer radically impacts the power of my ministry."

The huddle section of a VHS meeting likewise struck a felt need. "We had no idea how encouraged and helped L's and X's would feel when they met together twice a month," reports Pastor Dethmer. "The dynamics are explosive, and as a result leadership development is skyrocketing." Leaders usually spend an hour in their huddle time.

The skill section has also enhanced leader competency, especially after the VHS meetings increased in frequency from monthly (in the first year of Meta-Church transition) to semimonthly (every year thereafter). "When we met once a month," explains Pastor Dethmer, "we barely maintained our leaders. Now the support system is far more effective."

The L's conduct much of the skill training. That, combined with their visiting the small groups and meeting with the shepherds outside of VHS meetings, places a heavy work load on them.

The church staff invests much energy into seeking people with the spiritual maturity, necessary skills, and available time to serve in the labor-intensive role of an L. In 1990 Grace had sixteen L's for its adult small groups and twenty-seven L's for its learning center, a nursery-through-high-school graded program that runs during the worship service and maintains a ratio of one adult to every five children or youth.

The children's and youth ministry L's supervise some sixty learning center lay pastors (60 percent of whom are women). The adult ministry L's oversee almost seventy lay pastors (20 percent women, 15 percent husband-wife teams, and 65 percent men).

Pastor Dethmer reinforces the VHS concept each time he meets one-on-one with someone from Grace's leadership community. "From X's to L's to C's to D's, the first question I ask is, 'Who is your apprentice?' or 'How is your apprentice doing?' If anyone doesn't have an apprentice, I will ask to spend a few minutes praying together for whatever man or woman God is raising up for my leader to disciple. Multiplying cells comes as a result of developing apprentices."

Involvement Cap. Grace's most committed people can handle a maximum of five meetings a month, outside of Sunday worship. The typical small group meets three times a month, though some meet four. Two times is the minimum allowable. Thus cell leaders rarely have other areas of church involvement.

"Unless we limit the number of required meetings, church members will become so busy that they stop relating to lost people," explains Pastor Dethmer. "If they remain overcommitted, they'll next sacrifice their relationship with Christ. Then, finally, family relationships will go."

This busy pastor, who must oversee a fourteen-person staff, models the outreach focus of a healthy small group by leading one himself. His functioning both as an X and the leader of the D's creates slight structural complications. But the benefits are significant, especially on Sunday mornings, when he can make continual reference to what God is doing in the fellow members of his group.

Outreach Bias. Pastor Dethmer, spiritually gifted in evangelism, intentionally fills the group he leads with nonchurched non-Christians that he's met in nonreligious settings, such as by playing basketball. He wants to demonstrate to the church that side-door assimilation is a viable strategy with good promise of contributing to a greater evangelistic harvest than comes from front-door contacts alone.

As of 1990, some 90 percent of the people in small groups hadn't yet begun a side-door ministry with lost friends and acquaintances. Instead, they were growing by picking up church people. Grace Fellowship Church emulates the seeker-friendly style of worship service popularized by Willow Creek Community Church (*see* Chapter 2). Thus, with a number of nonbelievers frequenting Grace (up to 65 percent of Sunday-attendance growth), small groups can be evangelistic while fishing largely "in-house."

The question remains whether groups can be effective in side-door evangelism no matter what the spiritual gift of the X, Xa, or H (host) of the group. Peter Wagner has long indicated, for example, that he believes about 10 percent of the Body of Christ has the gift of evangelism. My observation of Paul Yonggi Cho's church in Korea is that home-cell leaders can *do the work of an evangelist*, regardless of the gift mix of the cell's leadership.

As the role and number of Xa apprentices increase, their activities will likewise enhance the corporate mind-set toward evangelism through the friendship networks of neighborhoods, marketplaces, and workplaces.

New Directions. In mid-1990 Pastor Dethmer accepted a call to serve on the pastoral staff at Willow Creek Community Church. The publication of this book follows closely on the heels of Grace's pastoral transition. Further trend analysis will need to wait until a new senior pastor can settle into his own ministry style.

Grace Fellowship Church demonstrates a widespread ownership of the Meta-Church vision. Yet according to Pastor Dethmer, the 1990 attendance of 1,400 doesn't yet comprise a full-blown example of a Meta-Church. "It takes years to reach the level of spontaneous combustion that I understand a Meta-Church to represent," he explains. "We are a well-organized, small-group ministry with a smoothly oiled system of leadership. We finally have more trained X's than available I's (potential cell membership) from our front-door contacts. Those circumstances make us ready for an attendance explosion. Leaders get hungry as piranha, and they begin nibbling for recruits in their neighborhoods and at church fishing ponds. In other words, they become prayerfully voracious to win people for their groups. Then spontaneous combustion occurs, fed by side-door growth."

Grace Fellowship Church prizes its gift-based, lay-driven one-another ministries. People are excited about the decentralized approach toward church life. Lay leaders have become the most-important ministry persons in the church. The church's purpose statement of loving

Christ, relating biblically, and maximizing giftedness has become, thanks to its small-group ministry, the core value of the movement.

"They Said It Couldn't Be Done"

Reverend Dale Galloway believes that one of the world's most foolish and limiting statements was uttered in 1898 by the director of the United States Patent Office: "Everything that can be invented has been invented."

In 1972, this pastor, then thirty-three, had no funds and no core group. But he and his wife nevertheless launched a new church in a rainy drive-in theater in Portland, Oregon. By 1990, Sunday worship attendance averaged 6,000 (three services on Sunday and one on Saturday night). In addition, more than 450 home-based small fellowship groups met weekly, each shepherded by a trained lay pastor. These small-group shepherds, 60–70 percent of whom are women, make about 15,000 contacts in their weekly ministries.

Pastor Galloway and New Hope Community Church (briefly introduced in Chapter 6), thrive on believing God for the impossible. As pioneers and pacesetters in developing need-meeting ministries led by laypeople, their goal is to have 100,000 members by the year 2000. They burn with an eagerness to emulate Jesus' mission of seeking and saving the lost (Luke 19:10) in Portland, where they calculate only one out of ten people are active members of any church. They insist that the time is ripe for different segments of God's people to build churches of 100,000-plus in every major city across North America.

Pastor Galloway grew up in Ohio, where his father was a district superintendent of some 150 churches. "My dad and I could not understand," he comments, "why year after year the vast majority of these churches showed no growth in membership. Something inside me said, *It's God's will for churches to grow. What's wrong?*"

Upon graduation from seminary, in 1963, Pastor Galloway discovered that church growth is a lot easier to talk about than to produce! After pastoring three churches while immersing himself in Scripture and prayer, he found the key God used to produce the 28 percent annual growth rate represented by New Hope.

In short, he discovered the principles we here describe as Meta-Church, which he terms the "church with 20/20 vision," taken from

Acts 20:20's reference to large group meetings and house-to-house ministry.[1] Lay pastors (X's) and lay-pastor trainees (Xa's) oversee Tender Loving Care groups (cell groups), which meet in homes. These men and women, in turn, receive careful training and supervision from full-time district pastors (D's) and from salaried or volunteer assistant pastors (L's). All these people gather for training and inspiration (VHS) every week: on Wednesday mornings (20 percent of the leadership), Wednesday evenings (40 percent), or Sunday evenings (40 percent).

The net result is "an organization with no internal limits to its ability to keep expanding," according to Pastor Galloway. "The 20/20 vision is for pastors and church leaders who want to charge ahead in multiplying God's church on an exponential curve!"

Pastor Galloway preaches an inspiring, positive message of hope in Jesus Christ. His spiritual gifts include evangelism and leadership. He sets the tone for conversion growth by leading the membership classes, in which 60 percent of the participants typically receive the Lord Jesus Christ as personal Savior. He also leads the church board, a self-perpetuating session of sixteen people of faith and vision whose budgetary and policy-making oversight makes ministry possible for everyone else.

At the same time he attributes the church's success rate to the Tender Loving Care groups. "We view every TLC group not only as a point of entry but as the fence that keeps our members healthy, happy, and in the church," he says. He summarizes the belonging and caring of cell ministry as "the essence of heart-to-heart fellowship." Unless people are brought into this kind of group, "They'll leave within two or three years, no matter how good the preaching, teaching, or music," he says.

Children's ministries have likewise been modeled on a TLC concept. Teachers, called lay pastors, gather weekly for guidance and inspiration along the same VHS pattern as leaders of adult TLC groups. On Sunday mornings the children's programming is age graded, much like traditional Sunday schools. During the week, a number of "Positive Action TLC's" focus on specific types of children: those from broken homes, those whose parents suffer with a codependent addiction, and so on.

Pastor Galloway's visionary approach to New Hope has been strongly influenced by such world Christian leaders as Paul Yonggi

Cho and Robert Schuller. Yet he doesn't consider them (or himself) to be unique. "They simply have dreamed bigger dreams, made the decision to 'go for it,' and daily cooperated with the Holy Spirit in making it a reality," he explains. "Great people are ordinary humans who become possessed with a cause greater than they are."

For Pastor Galloway, that enormous aim is observable in small units: nurture-based cell groups that grow and then multiply in number. His church started with one, but is pushing toward having six thousand such groups. At present about two-thirds of those involved in the groups also attend the corporate worship services; some go to other churches and some go nowhere—yet!

Two decades ago, advisers warned Pastor Galloway that no one could start a nondenominational church in Portland, without people or financial backing. Yet with Christ's help, he's done it—and he continues to lead New Hope Community Church across all potential barriers of growth.

Ever aware of how many people need the Lord, Pastor Galloway lives out his maxim: "No more business as usual!"

13
Enter the Future With Eyes Wide Open

Throughout *Prepare Your Church for the Future* I've referred to Pastor Paul Yonggi Cho, of Seoul, Korea. In 1979 he led Yoido Full Gospel Church to an average weekly attendance of more than 100,000 people. Historians will long remember this milestone, which had not been passed, or even approached, in the two millennia of the Christian era.

Many books and articles have described Pastor Cho's methods and theology. Thousands of Western Christians have traveled to Seoul to witness this outstanding ministry and attest to its integrity and effectiveness.

Yet in all of North America, only a half dozen prominent examples of a Cho-type church have emerged, and to date no Canadian or American church comes remotely close to its spiritual power or size. In fact, the Seoul church is bigger, at 650,000, than the largest 100 churches in North America all taken together!

The North American failure to successfully adopt Cho's model or to experience his successes usually receives one of three explanations:

- Korean culture allows for a stronger centralized leader than North American culture does; therefore it can't be done here.
- Korean people, as survivors of a recent war, are more susceptible to the gospel and to spiritual leadership than are North Americans; therefore it can't be done until after a war here.
- Koreans pray more fervently than affluent North American believers; therefore it won't be done here until or unless we pay the price in prayer.

I've concluded that only the third proposition is true. Prayerlessness does indeed distinguish us from our Korean counterparts.

But not all praying Korean churches are as fruitful as Dr. Cho's. To discover the secret of that particular church, we must look further than spiritual exercise, while never losing sight of the need for it.

I believe that North Americans can't adapt Dr. Cho's vision because we're stuck. Our theory of reality blinds us from discerning a form of ministry suitable for this generation. We need to discover—or better recover from Scripture—new rules of structure, method, and thinking that will open doors to effective church leadership.

That new paradigm is called the Meta-Church.

The Fire Within My Bones

A strange thing happened years ago when my wife, Grace, and one of our daughters, Babbie, were in our pediatrician's office awaiting a checkup. As the doctor entered the room, our three-year-old stretched out on the examining table and closed her eyes, keeping them shut throughout most of the examination.

Grace looked at Babbie and then at the doctor. "She's making me go away," he explained. "As long as she keeps her eyes closed, she can pretend that I'm not here."

What a parable of human existence! Refuse to observe what's going on, busy yourself, and make believe the changes all around needn't affect you. That's the easiest course for most people and churches to take.

Fortunately, many men and women in church leadership have purposed to enter the future with both eyes wide open. They're realizing that for our own spiritual health and survival, we must change.

This book's sketch of the Meta-Church, when combined with the exciting knowledge that hundreds of churches are already marching to the Meta-Church drumbeat, may prove to be dangerous to the status quo of conventional churches.

My colleagues and I have invested more than ten years so far in distinguishing the patterns purported in Meta-Church theory and then testing different aspects in a variety of settings. The resources listed above can provide an A to Z perspective on almost any dimension of the Meta-Church. But North America has yet to see the magnitude of ministry that might be unleashed by full-scale Meta-Church.

Scripture repeatedly affirms that God desires to redeem the human race from the power and penalty of sin. Jesus came to bring salvation. The Holy Spirit remains among and within us to assure our understanding of the truth, guide us in ministry, and provide adequate life-changing power. The church, in all its frailty and division, still upholds Christ's light to as many as can see it.

Yet almost every community contains a population of unreached people that continues to enlarge in unprecedented numbers. How can our merciful God use the arms of this generation's churches to bring multitudes to faith and love?

As a consultant to church leaders in more than five dozen denominations, I've listened to the heartbeat of many executives, pastors, and laypeople. They observe in some churches, new and old, large and small, wonderful achievements of a graceful God at work through a loving people. They likewise recognize in other churches despair, unmet needs, abysmal ignorance, and a woeful shortfall of faith.

This mosaic of contrasts creates a sickly universal church, too lame and blind to be an effective agent of redemption for its master. Carnal zeal dilutes incredible blessing. Passive indifference dulls gloriously changed lives. Noble purposes faint into actionless words. Smug satisfaction blocks the prayer that could release heaven's powers. Little wonder that the majority of this continent's churches are in nongrowth modes unable to keep pace with the population.

This book is my contribution toward opening the eyes of leaders everywhere. It has mapped some of the strategies required to multiply ministry and spiritual nurture to the 5 billion individuals on this planet. It challenges readers to institute in their churches a different model of social architecture. It calls for North American Christians to shift our mental paradigms so we can break out of our current ineffective patterns. It outlines practices and principles crucial to reaping an increased harvest of souls. It affirms that we can indeed experience the truly massive spiritual growth evidenced on other continents.

Our generation possesses opportunities that can extend beyond most people's wildest dreams. Technological advances, population growth, governmental restructuring, and global ecological partnerships are opening a future unlike anything previously encountered. Our responsibility for wise stewardship of today's possibilities must drive each of us to our knees. Only with God's direction will we reap the spiritual harvest next door and around the globe.

Some churches will continue to be effective without implementing many of the changes suggested in *Prepare Your Church for the Future*. It may not be within the will of the Creator to disturb these havens of tradition. Perhaps their members will find limited insight and assistance here, even if the old models best serve their particular scope of ministry.

Others may put this book aside because the loss of the familiar causes too much discomfort.

Yet for those who seek to multiply ministry in the context of today's ever-changing circumstances of life, the message of this book stands as a Magna Charta. Present ministry assumptions and structures must be reevaluated to detect hindrances to new solutions, to new leadership, to new organizational patterns, and to new places of ministry.

Receptive readers will discern a prophetic call to the great challenge of our times. They will endure its uncomfortable implications. They, with me, will sense a compulsion from God. They will engage in ministry enlightened by a vision that becomes a fire burning in their bones.

Such a conviction has kindled a divine mission from which my soul can find no rest.

Resources

Over the last few years, more than 250 large churches (with weekly worship attendances from 700 to 10,000) have sent their pastors and key lay leaders to a three-day consultation event. After gaining a thorough understanding of the Meta-Church paradigm, they develop an action plan that fits their church circumstances.

In addition, hundreds of other churches have sent delegates to Meta-Zone™ seminars that focus on various components of the Meta-Church. These include "Training Lay Pastors to Lead Home Groups" (Green Zone), Making Celebration-Size Events Come Alive (Red Zone), and "Reaching the Unchurched Through Felt-Need Events" (Yellow Zone). Magazine articles, monthly cassette programs, and other communication tools are likewise disseminating insights on different aspects of Meta-Church implementation.

Meanwhile, a number of regional centers designed to develop leadership for ministry are being formed. An Electronic District of the Future now exists in our Southern California offices where modems, FAXes, and specialized computer programs are beginning to monitor the progress of exemplar churches that have agreed to serve as laboratories in which others can observe and learn.

Most important, disciples are being made! Tens of thousands of parishioners in large churches (800 plus) and multi-staff churches (400 plus) are being led to increase their spiritual maturity and impact for Christ through effective cell multiplication. Thousands of new churches, piloted by pastors recently tutored in Meta-Church principles, are poising themselves for new-member growth that will potentially touch hundreds of thousands of unchurched people.

The organization—one of the largest of its kind in the world—sponsoring their dissemination of training and technology is the Los Angeles-based Charles E. Fuller Institute of Evangelism and Church Growth, sponsored jointly by the Fuller Evangelistic Association and Fuller Theological Seminary School of World Missions. Its staff of thirty works from an office in Pasadena and a warehouse in Glendora. Its not-for-profit mission is "to provide the highest quality in-service training possible for church executives, pastors, staff and laypeople."

Together with a consortium of nationally recognized speakers and writers, the Charles E. Fuller Institure has developed a wide array of resources through seminars, audiocassettes, videocassettes, and books. Here's a sampling:

Seminar Topics

The Meta-Zone™ seminars and Meta-Cluster Consultation (described on the previous page) offer in-depth exposure to various dimensions of Meta-Church research and application.

Another well-known group of seminars equips pastors and lay leaders to improve their leadership skills and overcome obstacles to growth. Among the current offerings: "Pastor's Toolbox," "Assimilation: Closing the Back Door," "How to Break the 100-200 Barrier," 'How to Break the 200 Barrier," "Beyond 400" and "Beyond 800."

Other popular seminars focus on spiritual warfare and spiritual disciplines. Present listings include "Developing Prayer Ministries in Your Local Church" and "Prayer Strategies for Taking Your City."

In order to help leaders stay abreast of church-related social developments, the Charles E. Fuller Institute offers seminars on a number of culturally current topics, such as "Recovery Ministries"and "Baby Boomers."

Church planters receive training in the latest research and strategies through such seminars as "New Church Incubator" and "How to Plant a Church."

Finally, one of the best-received seminars, "Pastor's Personal Life," offers meaningful assistance with the special pressures and needs of clergy marriages.

Self-Study Kits

Assimilation (incorporating new people into the life of your church).

Baby Boomers (recognizing the identity and needs of America's unchurched baby-boomer generation).

Church Planter's Toolkit (clarifying your vision, developing your strategy, and starting churches that reproduce).

Conflict and Change (learning to manage change and effectively mediate conflict).

Discovering Spiritual Gifts (introducing believers to a small group-based method of spiritual gift discovery).

How to Have a Prayer Ministry (discovering new avenues of renewal, personal growth, and power in ministry).

How to Lead and Manage the Local Church (organizing oneself, learning to delegate, building a team, and setting goals).

Lay Ministry (communicating vision and motivating laypeople for ministry).

Networking (helping Christians identify their spiritual gifts, calling, desires, temperament, and talents).

Stewardship (training your people to grasp the benefits of lifestyle stewardship).

"The Phone's for You!" (using a telemarketing strategy suitable for both new and existing churches).

Ushers and Greeters (developing a successful usher-and-greeter ministry).

What Visitors See (helping your church become more "visitor friendly").

Your Church Can Be Healthy (diagnosing the baseline issues and present condition of your church).

Monthly Cassette Programs

Pastor's Update, with more than 3,000 subscribers, is a monthly tape program and newsletter that capsulizes cutting-edge insights from the best of today's pastors and growth consultants.

MetaFacts, the newest tape program, offers fresh ideas and motivational inspiration for pastors who are implementing the most significant ministry model of our time.

Book Topics

Church growth, lay ministry, small church, church management, finances, leadership and motivation, spiritual gifts, church planting, supervision of church planters, evangelism, prayer, multiple staff, vision casting, codependency, addiction recovery, and more.

To order a free catalog or to inquire further about The Meta-Church Project™, call 1-800-MAP-META. Or write to The Center for the Development of Leadership for Ministry™, P.O. Box 5407, Diamond Bar, CA 91765-5407. Or use either of these twenty-four-hour FAX numbers: 1-800-289-6129 or 1-818-449-6129.

Source Notes

Chapter 1: Prepare for Future Shock

1. John Naisbitt, *Megatrends: Ten New Directions Transforming Our Lives* (New York: Warner Books, 1982).

2. John Naisbitt and Patricia Aburdene, *Megatrends 2000: Ten New Directions for the 1990s* (New York: William Morrow and Co., 1990).

3. Lyle Schaller, *It's a Different World* (Nashville, Tenn., Abingdon Press, 1987).

4. David McKenna, *Mega Truth: The Church in the Age of Information* (San Bernardino, Calif.: Here's Life Publishers, 1986).

5. Joel Arthur Barker, *Discovering the Future: The Business of Paradigms* (St. Paul, Minn.: Infinity Limited Institute Press, 1988).

6. Howard A. Snyder with Daniel V. Runyon, *Foresight: Ten Major Trends That Will Dramatically Affect the Future of Christians and the Church* (Nashville, Tenn.: Thomas Nelson Publishers, 1986).

7. Peter F. Drucker, *The Age of Discontinuity: Guidelines to Our Changing Society* (New York: Harper & Row, 1968, 1969).

8. Peter F. Drucker, *The New Realities: In Government and Politics; in Economics and Business; in Society and World View* (New York: Harper & Row, 1989).

9. Henry Mintzberg, *Structure in Fives: Designing Effective Organizations* (Englewood Cliffs, N.J.: Prentice-Hall, 1983).

10. Tom Peters, *Thriving on Chaos* (New York: Alfred A. Knopf, Inc., 1987).

11. "The World's Urban Explosion," *National Geographic* 166 (August 1984), no. 2, 180.

12. U.S. Census Bureau, cited in *U.S. News & World Report*, 2/19/90, as quoted in *Leadership* (Fall 1990), 129.

13. "The World's Urban Explosion," *National Geographic* 166 (August 1984), no. 2, 180.

14. ibid.

15. ibid.

16. Frank R. Tillapaugh, *Unleashing the Church* (Ventura, Calif.: Regal Books, 1982), 224 pages.

Chapter 2: Tally What You Inherited

1. George Sweeting, comp., *Great Quotes and Illustrations* (Waco, Texas: Word, 1985), 219.

Chapter 3: Rattle the Cage Around Your Zoo

1. The terms *cat-size church* and *dog-size church* were coined and popularized by Lyle Schaller and Arlin Rothauge.

2. John N. Vaughan, Megachurch Research Center, Southwest Baptist University, Bolivar, Mo., 65613 (417) 326-1773. Data used by permission.

3. *Ibid.*

4. See the extended discussion in Howard Snyder's *The Problem of Wineskins*, (Downers Grove, Ill., Inter-Varsity Press, 1976), 139–149.

Chapter 5: Consider the Meta Advantages

1. This paradigm comes from David Luecke's seminal book, *Evangelical Style and Lutheran Substance* (St. Louis, Mo.: Concordia Publishing House, 1988).

2. This model is adapted from Dan Reeves, *Always Advancing* (San Bernardino, Calif.: Here's Life Pubs., 1984).

3. The three size categories highlighted in this section were first described by Peter Wagner in *Your Church Can Grow*, rev. (Ventura, Calif.: Regal Books, 1984), 111–126.)

Chapter 9: Train Your Leaders Thoroughly

1. Reverend Warren Bird, who contributed heavily to the editing of this book while serving the Suffern Alliance Church, Suffern, New York, took the time to compile this list.

2. The Meta-Church defines five dimensions of care:

> *Primary.* A person in need of care can look to someone who has accepted responsibility for providing that first level of care. Examples: in a family between parent and child, in a small group between leader and member.
>
> *Mutual.* The peers of a member, usually in the context of a primary-care group, offer encouragement. Examples: sibling care in a family, small-group members who have permission to help one another.
>
> *Backup.* The caregiver receives assistance from a supervisor or coach who makes additional skills available to the care recipient through that person. Examples: a coach counseling a small-group leader on how to handle a situation, a consultant advising a pastor.
>
> *Referral.* The caregiver recommends appropriate community, mental health, or pastoral support resources. Examples: a small-group leader urging a member with chronic depression to go to a medical doctor for a physical examination, a small-group member urging a friend in the group to go to an accountant for financial advice about a prospective business deal.
>
> *Secondary.* The subject is in a caregiver's environment but has a stronger, primary-care connection somewhere else in the care giving system. Examples: the grandparents, aunts, and uncles in a family; the role of the choir to a small-group member.

Chapter 11: See Yourself as a Manager and Communicator

1. These role descriptions are copyright 1987 and 1988 by Carl F. George. Used by permission.

Chapter 12: Glean Insights From Others

1. A full account of the church's philosophy and practice appears in Dale E. Galloway, *20/20 Vision: How to Create a Successful Church,* rev. ed. (11731 S.E. Stevens Rd., Portland, Ore., 97266: Scott Publishing Co. 1986) 1988, 160 pages, hardcover.

Annotated Bibliography

Arn, Win, Carroll Nyquist, and Charles Arn. *Who Cares About Love?* Pasadena, Calif.: Church Growth Press, 1986.

Banks, Robert and Julia. *The Home Church: Regrouping the People of God for Community and Mission.* Sutherland, Australia: Albatross Books, 1986.

Barker, Joel Arthur. *Discovering the Future: The Business of Paradigms.* St. Paul, Minn.: Infinity Limited Institute Press, 1988. "While trends are important, they are almost always instigated by a paradigm shift. By understanding the ways paradigms change, we can better anticipate the future."

Barker, Steve, Judy Johnson, Jimmy Long, Rob Malone, and Ron Nicholas. *Small Group Leaders' Handbook.* Downers Grove, Ill.: Inter-Varsity Press, 1982.

Barker, Steve, and Judy Johnson, Rob Malone, Ron Nicholas, Doug Whallon. *Good Things Come in Small Groups.* Downers Grove, Ill.: Inter-Varsity Press, 1985.

Barna, Geroge. *The Frog in the Kettle: What Christians Need to Know about Life in the Year 2000.* Ventura, Calif.: Regal Books, 1990.

Barrett, Lois. *Building the House Church.* Scottdale, Penna.: Herald Press, 1986.

Bellah, Robert N., Richard Madsen, William M. Sullivan, Ann Swidler, and

Stephen M. Tipton. *Habits of the Heart: Individualism and Commitment in American Life.* New York: Harper & Row, 1985.

Bennis, Warren, and Burt Nanus. *Leaders: The Strategies for Taking Charge.* New York: Harper & Row, 1985.

Bennis, Warren. *On Becoming a Leader.* New York: Addison-Wesley, 1989.

Birch, George A. *The Deliverance Ministry.* Cathedral City, Calif.: Horizon House Publishers, 1988.

Blackburn, Bill, and Deana Mattingly Blackburn. *Caring in Times of Family Crisis.* Nashville, Tenn., 1987.

Brown, J. Douglas. *The Human Nature of Organizations.* New York: AMA-COM, 1973. Secular work that looks at the depersonalizing effects of technology and bigness and the misapplication of scientific approaches to human affairs that strip people of their dignity and lead to shoddy workmanship and resentment against all bureaucracies.

Cho, Dr. Paul Yonggi. *The Fourth Dimension.* Plainfield, N.J.: Logos International, 1979.

Cho, Paul Yonggi with Harold Hostetler. *Successful Home Cell Groups.* Plainfield, N.J.: Logos International, 1981.

Cho, Paul Y. with R. Whitney Manzano. *More Than Numbers.* Waco, Tex.: Word Books, 1984.

Cho, Paul Y. with R. Whitney Manzano. *Prayer: Key to Revival.* Waco, Tex.: Word Books, 1984.

Clark, Stephen B. *Building Christian Communities: Strategy for Renewing the Church.* Notre Dame, Ind.: Ave Maria Press, 1972. Roman Catholic in orientation, provides many helpful suggestions for developing Christ-centered communities to foster Christian life in all its members and leadership development from within.

Clinebell, Howard J., Jr. *The People Dynamic: Changing Self and Society Through Growth Groups.* New York: Harper & Row, 1972.

Coleman, Lyman. *Encyclopedia of Serendipity,* Littleton, Colo.: Serendipity House, 1976.

Coleman, Robert E. *The Master Plan of Discipleship.* Old Tappan, N.J.: Fleming H. Revell Co., 1987.

Coleman, Robert E., *The Master Plan of Evangelism.* Old Tappan, N.J.: Fleming H. Revell Co., 1964.

Davis, Stanley M. *Future Perfect.* New York: Addison-Wesley, 1987.

Dayton, Edward R. and Ted W. Engstom. *Strategy for Leadership.* Old Tappan, N.J.: Fleming H. Revell Co., 1979.

Dawson, John. *Taking Our Cities for God: How to Break Spiritual Strongholds.* Lake Mary, Fla.: Creation House, 1989.

Doering, Jeanne. *The Power of Encouragement: Discovering Your Ministry of Affirmation*. Chicago: Moody Press, 1983. The nature, methods, source, and results of encouragement. Features chapter discussions of eight methods of encouragement.

Drucker, Peter F. *The Age of Discontinuity: Guidelines to Our Changing Society*. New York: Harper & Row, 1968, 1969.

Drucker, Peter F. *Innovation and Entrepreneurship: Practice and Principles*. New York: Harper & Row, 1985.

Drucker, Peter F. *The New Realities: In Government and Politics; In Economics and Business; In Society and World View*. New York: Harper & Row, 1989.

Friedman, Edwin H. *Generation to Generation*. New York: The Guilford Press, 1985.

Galloway, Dale E. *Lay Pastor Training Manual for Successful Home Group Meetings*. Portland, Ore.: New Hope Community Church, n.d.

Galloway, Dale E. *20/20 Vision: How to Create a Successful Church*. Portland, Ore.: Scott Publishing Company, 1986. This is one book that accords closely with the principles of the Meta-Church, by a pastor who has been the most successful in applying the principles the Holy Spirit has displayed in Dr. Cho's church in Seoul, Korea, to a church in North America.

Garlow, James L. *Partners in Ministry: Laity and Pastors Working Together*. Kansas City, Mo.: Beacon Hill Press of Kansas City, 1981.

George, Carl and Robert Logan. *Leading and Managing Your Church*. Old Tappan, N.J.: Fleming H. Revell Co., 1987.

Getz, Gene A. *Building Up One Another*. Wheaton, Ill.: Victor Books, 1976. A discussion of twelve "one another" commands of the New Testament.

Gilbert, Larry. *Team Ministry*. Lynchburg, Va.: Church Growth Institute, 1987. Glossary. Extensive bibliography. This book is a practical discussion of the relationship of spiritual gifts to lay involvement and church growth. It contains a particularly good discussion of task-oriented spiritual gifts.

Goslin, Thomas S., II. *The Church Without Walls*. Pasadena, Calif.: Hope Publishing House, 1984. The church is not a building, but the company of the redeemed. Goslin suggests we place less emphasis upon church buildings, which often isolate our congregations from the world and the poor and tie up too much of our resources, limiting our ability to plant new churches and evangelize the world. He reflects upon his experience with the Community Church of Madrid, a church that determined from the beginning not to have a building of its own.

Grantham, Rudolph E. *Lay Shepherding*. Valley Forge, Penna.: Judson Press, 1980.

Hadaway, C. Kirk, Stuart A. Wright, and Francis M. DuBose. *Home Cell Groups and House Churches*. Nashville, Tenn.: Broadman Press, 1987.

Hallesby, O. *Prayer*. Minneapolis, Minn.: Augsburg Publishing House, 1931.

Harman, Willis W. *An Incomplete Guide to the Future*. New York: W. W. Norton Company, 1979. Secular futurism. Harman develops the thesis that we are undergoing a metamorphosis in society similar in extent and impact to former changes like the Industrial Revolution, but we have the advantage of identifying the essential characteristics of the transition while it is in process.

Harper, Michael. *Let My People Grow: Ministry and Leadership in the Church*. London: Hodder & Stoughton, 1977.

Haugk, Kenneth C. *Christian Caregiving—A Way of Life*. Minneapolis, Minn.: Augsburg Publishing House, 1984. Haugk is the founder and executive director of Stephen Ministries.

Haugk, Kenneth C. and William J. McKay. *Christian Caregiving—A Way of Life Leader's Guide*. Minneapolis, Minn.: Augsburg Publishing House, 1986.

Hipp, Jeanne. *How to Start and Grow Small Groups in Your Church*. Monrovia, Calif.: Church Growth, 1989.

Hosier, Helen. *How to Know When God Speaks*. Irvine, Calif.: Harvest House Publishers, 1980.

Hubbard, David Allan. *Unwrapping Your Spiritual Gifts*. Waco, Tex.: Word Books, 1985.

Hull, Bill. *The Disciple Making Church*. Old Tappan, N.J.: Fleming H. Revell Co., 1990.

Hull, Bill. *The Disciple Making Pastor*. Old Tappan, N.J.: Fleming H. Revell Co., 1988.

Hull, Bill. *Jesus Christ Disciple Maker*. Old Tappan, N.J.: Fleming H. Revell Co., 1984, 1990.

Hurston, John W. and Karen Hurston. *Caught in the Web*. Anaheim, Calif.: Church Growth International and Mountain Press, 1977.

Hurston, John, comp. *Home Fellowships International Training Manual*. Vol. 2. Dallas, Tex.: Word of Faith World Outreach Center, 1986.

Jacks, Bob and Betty, with Ron Wormser, Sr. *Your Home, a Lighthouse*. San Bernardino, Calif.: Churches Alive! 1986.

Jacobsen, Marion Leach. *Crowded Pews and Lonely People*. Wheaton, Ill.: Tyndale House Publishers, 1972.

Kets de Vries, Manfred F. R., and Danny Miller. *Unstable at the Top: Inside the Troubled Organization*. New York: New American Library, 1987.

Kim, Ki Dong. *Theories of Church Growth Centered on Sung Rak Baptist Church*. Seoul, Korea: Berea Press, 1986.

Kincaid, Ron. *A Celebration of Disciple-Making*. Wheaton, Ill.: Victor Books, 1990.

Kuhn, Thomas. *The Structure of Scientific Revolutions*. 2d ed. Chicago: University of Chicago Press, 1962, 1970.

Lavin, Ronald J. *You Can Grow In a Small Group*. Lima, Ohio: C.S.S. Publishing Co., 1976.

Lea, Larry. *Could You Not Tarry One Hour?* Altamonte Springs, Fla.: Creation House, 1987. How to use the Lord's Prayer as an outline for an hour of daily prayer.

Lea, Larry. *The Hearing Ear: Learning to Listen to God*. Altamonte Springs, Fla.: Creation House, 1988. How to develop your spiritual hearing by removing hindrances, using God's "hearing aids," using the Lord's Prayer, testing, then obeying what is heard.

Lee, Bernard J. and Michael A. Cowan. *Dangerous Memories: House Churches and Our American Story*. Kansas City, Mo.: Sheed & Ward, 1986.

Logan, Robert E. *Beyond Church Growth*. Old Tappan, N.J.: Fleming H. Revell Co., 1989. Ten key principles, including emphasis upon vision, pastoral leadership, culturally relevant philosophy of ministry, disciple making, expanding network of cell groups, developing and resourcing leaders, and mobilizing believers according to spiritual gifts, to stimulate not only local church growth but also to plant churches that reproduce.

Luecke, David. *Evangelical Style and Lutheran Substance: Facing America's Mission Challenge*. St. Louis, Mo.: Concordia Publishing House, 1988. Discusses the village and the camp styles in American churches. Seeks an answer to how older churches can renew their evangelistic impact and grow by borrowing styles used successfully by the newer churches.

Maney, Thomas. *Basic Communities: A Practical Guide for Renewing Neighborhood Churches*. Minneapolis, Minn.: Winston Press, 1984.

Mason, David E. *Voluntary Nonprofit Enterprise Management*. New York: Plenum Publishing Corp., 1984. Secular work written by an author who is sympathetic to and acquainted with churches and spiritual concerns, though they are not addressed directly in the book. Centers upon the business model, careful goal setting, and effective use of resources. Gives wise counsel concerning the life cycle of organizations.

McKenna, David. *Mega Truth*. San Bernardino, Calif.: Here's Life Publishers, 1986.

Meadows, Donella H., Dennis L. Meadows, Jorgen Randers, and William W. Behrens III. *The Limits to Growth*. New York: Universe Books, 1974.

Mintzberg, Henry, *Structure in Fives: Designing Effective Organizations*. Englewood Cliffs, N.J.: Prentice-Hall, 1983. Five different forms or con-

figurations organizations take: the simple structure, the machine bureaucracy, the professional bureaucracy, the divisionalized form, and the
adhocracy. The book's opening illustration suggests that a group of five
people is the limit for effective accomplishment without the imposition of
some form of structure or control.

Naisbitt, John. *Megatrends: Ten New Directions Transforming Our Lives.*
New York: Warner Books, 1982.

Naisbitt, John, and Patricia Aburdene. *Megatrends 2000.* New York: William
Morrow & Co., 1990.

Navigators, The. *How to Lead Small Group Bible Studies: A Navigator Guide.*
Colorado Springs, Colo.: Navpress, 1982.

Neighbour, Ralph W., Jr., comp. *Future Church.* Nasville, Tenn.: Broadman
Press, 1980.

Neighbour, Ralph W., Jr. *The Shepherd's Guidebook.* Houston, Tex.: Touch
Outreach Ministries, 1989. Though disparging any hope for reaching and
changing the traditional church, this is a mature book written from vast
experience in small-group shepherding and is crammed with practical ideas
and insight.

Neighbour, Ralph W., Jr. *Where Do We Go From Here? A Guidebook for the
Cell Group Church.* Houston, Tex.: Touch Outreach Ministries, 1990. An
excellent overview of how and why to build a "cell driven" church.

Neighbour, Ralph W., Jr., and Cal Thomas. *Target-Group Evangelism.* Nashville, Tenn.: Broadman Press, 1975.

Newton, Tom. *Go For It!* Fresno, Calif.: The Small Group Network, 1989.

Newton, Tom. *Let's Worship.* Fresno, Calif.: The Small Group Network, n.d.

Newton, Tom. *Level I Training Event Manual.* Fresno, Calif.: The Small
Group Network, 1987, 1988.

Newton, Tom. *Worship: A Ten Lesson Series.* Fresno, Calif.: The Small
Group Network, n.d.

Noon, Scott C. *Building Attendance in Your Youth Ministry.* Loveland, Colo.:
Group Books, 1989.

Olsen, Charles M. *The Base Church.* Atlanta, Ga.: Forum House Publishers,
1973. The small-group alternative to edifice-centered, clergy-dominated
institutions. Building church structures upon a network of interdependent,
small, base groups is vital to the renewal of the church. The new forms can
be constructed within, alongside, or outside the parish congregation.

Ott, E. Stanley. *The Vibrant Church: A People Building Plan for Congregational Health.* Ventura, Calif.: Regal Books, 1989.

Pastor's Planning Workbook. Part 3 "Program Design." Pasadena, Calif.:
Charles E. Fuller Institute, 1981.

Peace, Richard. *Small Group Evangelism.* Downers Grove, Ill.: InterVarsity Press, 1985.

Peters, Ted. *Futures, Human and Divine.* Atlanta, Ga.: John Knox Press, 1978. A critical examination of secular futurology from the perspective of Christian theology.

Reeves, R. Daniel, and Ronald Jenson. *Always Advancing: Modern Strategies for Church Growth.* San Bernardino, Calif.: Here's Life Publishers, 1984. Peter Wagner calls this book "a basic church growth primer, the book you will want to give away as a concise introduction to the field." Insightful material on "people flow," paradigm and paradigm shifts, philosophy of ministry, and typologies. Extensive bibliography, index of persons, index of subjects.

Reid, Tommy, with Doug Brendel. *The Exploding Church.* Plainfield, N.J.: Logos International, 1979.

Rothauge, Arlin. *Sizing Up the Church for New Member Ministry.* Washington, D.C.: Alban Inst., nd.

Sale, Kirkpatrick. *Human Scale.* New York: Coward, McCann & Geoghegan, 1980.

Schaller, Lyle E. *It's a Different World.* Nashville, Tenn.: Abingdon, 1987.

Schaller, Lyle E. *Understanding Tomorrow.* Nashville, Tenn.: Abingdon, 1976.

Schmitt, Abraham and Dorothy. *When a Congregation Cares: A New Approach to Crisis Ministry.* Scottdale, Penna.: Herald Press, 1986.

Schuller, Robert H. *Your Church Has a Fantastic Future!* Ventura, Calif.: Regal Books, 1986.

Schumacher, E. F. *Small Is Beautiful: Economics as if People Mattered.* New York: Harper & Row, 1973.

Simpson, Charles. *The Challenge to Care.* Ann Arbor, Mich.: Servant Publications, 1986.

Slater, Michael. *Stretcher Bearers.* Ventura, Calif.: Regal Books, 1985.

Snyder, Howard A. *The Community of the King.* Downers Grove, Ill.: InterVarsity Press, 1977.

Snyder, Howard A. *The Problem of Wineskins.* Downers Grove, Ill.: InterVarsity Press, 1975.

Snyder, Howard A., with Daniel V. Runyon. *Foresight.* Nashville, Tenn.: Thomas Nelson Publishers, 1986.

Spiritual Gifts Mobilization: "Leader's Workbook." Pasadena, Calif.: Charles E. Fuller Institute, 1987.

Stanley, Charles. *How to Listen to God.* Nashville, Tenn.: Thomas Nelson, 1985.

Stedman, Ray C. *Body Life.* Glendale, Calif.: Regal Books, 1972.

Steyne, Philip M. *Gods of Power*. Houston, Tex.: Touch Publications, 1989.

Stott, John R. *One People*. Old Tappan, N.J.: Fleming H. Revell Co., 1982.

Tillapaugh, Frank R. *Unleashing the Church*. Ventura, Calif.: Regal Books, 1982.

Towns, Elmer L. *The Bright Future of the Sunday School*. Minneapolis, Minn.: F.C. Publications, 1969.

Towns, Elmer L., John N. Vaughan, and David J. Seifert. *The Complete Book of Church Growth*. Wheaton, Ill.: Tyndale House Publishers, 1981.

Tregoe, Benjamin B., and John W. Zimmerman, Ronald A. Smith, Peter M. Tobia. *Vision in Action: Putting a Winning Strategy to Work*. New York: Simon & Schuster, 1989. How to transform vision into strategy. Though oriented to business interests, includes insights derived from a study of nineteen organizations, including a Christian university. Includes a chapter "Communicating Vision Through the Ranks."

Ver Straten, Charles A. *How to Start Lay-Shepherding Ministries*. Grand Rapids, Mich.: Baker Book House, 1983. Aimed at equipping lay people to do the work of pastoral care.

Wagner, C. Peter, with Win Arn and Elmer Towns. *Church Growth: State of the Art*. Wheaton, Ill.: Tyndale House Publishers, 1986. Features a Who's Who in church growth section, glossary, annotated bibliography, and index.

Wagner, C. Peter. *Leading Your Church to Growth*. Ventura, Calif.: Regal Books, 1984.

Wagner, C. Peter. *Spiritual Power and Church Growth*. Altamonte Springs, Fla.: Strang Communications Co., 1986.

Wagner, C. Peter. *Your Church Can Grow*. Ventura, Calif.: Regal Books, 1976, 1984.

Wagner-Modified Houts Questionnaire. Pasadena, Calif.: Charles E. Fuller Institute, 1978, 1985.

Walton, William B. with Mel Lorentzen. *The New Bottom Line*. New York: Harper & Row, 1986.

Warren, Richard, with William A. Shell. *12 Dynamic Bible Study Methods for Individuals or Groups*. Wheaton, Ill.: Victor Books, 1981. This fine handbook on Bible-study methods is especially helpful on the character quality and biographical methods of Bible study.

Wilson, Charles R. *Under Authority: Supervision and Church Leadership*. Arvada, Colo.: Jethro Publications, 1989.

Wollen, Albert J. *Miracles Happen in Group Bible Study*. Glendale, Calif.: Regal Books, 1976.

Womack, David A. *The Pyramid Principle of Church Growth*. Minneapolis, Minn.: Bethany Fellowship, 1977. Written as a layman's guide to church growth. The present concept of sanctuary-centered churches is not capable of fulfilling the Great Commission. Future success in reaching the harvest lies not within the walls of the church building, but out in the streets and the houses where the people are. To grow a pyramid, its base must be enlarged. The base for church growth is lay leadership.

Yeakley, Flavil R., Jr., ed. Howard W. Norton, Don E. Vinzant, Gene Vinzant. *The Discipling Dilemma: A Study of the Discipling Movement Among the Churches of Christ.* Nashville, Tenn.: Gospel Advocate Company, 1988.

Index

Listings in italics indicate entries in charts.